Ka'nu Culture

Steve West

Outrigger Canoeing

Batini Books

KANU – the German word for canoe was adopted in the language of Papua New Guinea as a result of contact with German missionaries. The word is officially incorporated into Neo-Melanesian or Pidgin English.

CULTURE – a particular form, stage or type of intellectual development or civilization; improvement by (mental or physical) training.

AUTHOR & PUBLISHER
Steve West

Special thanks to Todd Bradley for his untiring support and encouragement of my vision and of Ka'nu Culture. Also to his wife Chris and children Brendan and Christian for accepting me into their family during my trips to Hawaii.

To Greg Moss and his boat handling skills in allowing me to get some great photographs. To Walter Guild for his enormous encouragement and support. And to everyone who has contributed their energy to these contents.

Mahalo Nui Loa for your spirit of aloha and for contributing so much to this second volume.

EDITOR & COPY EDITOR
Rosie West

CONTRIBUTING AUTHORS
Kris Kjeldsen (New Zealand)
Di Barr (Australia)

CONTRIBUTING PHOTOGRAPHERS
Barry Alsop (Australia)
New Zealand photos courtesy of Kris Kjeldsen
Jason Somerville-Kimlin (Australia)

All photographs are the work of Steve West unless otherwise acknowledged.

Kanu-Culture is published on an annual basis at the beginning of each year. Contributions in the form of type written articles and photographs for consideration are most welcome. Please address all correspondence to:

PO Box 506, Maroochydore
Sunshine Coast, Australia, Qld 4558.
Telephone & Fax (074) 79 1327
International # 61 74 79 1327

Internet

email address: kanu@ozemail.com.au

World Wide Web (Home Page)

http://www.ozemail.com.au/~kanu

Copyright © Steve West 1996

West, S. R.
Ka'nu - Culture 1996
ISBN 0 9586554 0 5

DESIGN & PRE-PRESS
Steve & Rosie West

PUBLISHING CONSULTANT
Tony Izzard

PRINTING
PH Productions Pte Ltd, Singapore

MAHALO NUI LOA ALSO TO
Mike Atwood (Hawaii) Torey Brown (Oregon) Corrina Gage (New Zealand) Ron Grabbe (Australia) Walter Guild (Hawaii) Nolan Hendricks (Guam) Bud Hohl (California) Mary-Jane Kahanamoku (Hawaii) Greg Moss (Hawaii) Bev & Waitai Murray (New Zealand) Vicki Murray (New Zealand) Jason Somerville-Kimlin (Australia) Mike Tongg (Hawaii) Mary Serrao (Hawaii). *Also to Bobby Woods, Dana Point OCC California who was the artist responsible for the capsize drawings in the '95 issue of KC.*

COVER PIC: "Four Determined Paddlers" by Raymond Helgeson, resident artist of the Big Island of Hawaii.

Contents

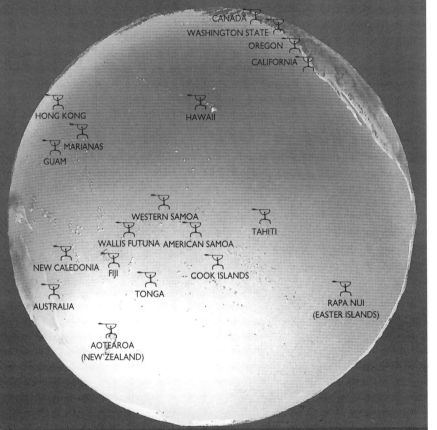

Planet Outrigger

Powerful imagery of the vast watery playground
around which inhabitants of the Pacific Rim and Pacific Islands live, work and play.
Outrigger canoeing is historically and culturally indigenous to this region,
but little by little, bit by bit, its appeal is becoming more universal, spreading
beyond this aquatic expanse, across Canada, North America and into Europe.
Planet outrigger is growing on a daily basis as its appeal spreads far and wide
to some of the most unlikely spots on the planet. From obscurity to familiarity it rises
creating a sense of community across the globe.

Welcome to Planet Outrigger...

...a message from the author and publisher.

Dear Reader

In this one small page which represents one two-hundredth or thereabouts of the total contents of this book, I speak on behalf of myself – after all the other pages are for you.

My thanks for all the letters, faxes and vocal messages of support we have received from around the world – from Hawaii and Tahiti, New Zealand and the Easter Islands, California and Canada, Guam and Australia, New Caledonia and Fiji and even as far away as France and England.

Outrigger canoeing continues to enjoy rapid growth around the Pacific and Pacific Rim, but perhaps the biggest surprise is the growing interest in European countries such as England, France, Germany, Hungary and Sweden. And now South Africa where an outrigger association has recently been formed.

Rumours are that outrigger canoe racing will soon be happening on the east coast of America and it is expected to spread fairly rapidly from there to the warmer areas of Florida and the Caribbean. With phenomenal interest in solo outrigger canoes the potential for growth is enormous as the sport can now appeal to an ever increasing broader cross-section of people.

I trust that you find pleasure in our second volume of Ka'nu Culture and enjoyment in participation on the many different levels outrigger canoeing provides, be it physical, mental, spiritual or cultural there is something for everyone. The more of these aspects you embrace, the more fulfilling your involvement will become.

Our family is growing daily.

Aloha
Steve West

A MESSAGE FROM THE KA'NU CULTURE PRESERVATION SOCIETY.
BUY YOUR OWN COPY. THERE'S PLENTY FOR EVERYONE. REFUSE TO LEND YOUR COPY OUT. CLUBS AND ASSOCIATIONS, DO NOT ADOPT THE PRACTICE OF PURCHASING ONE COPY FOR YOUR ENTIRE MEMBERSHIP. ENCOURAGE YOUR MEMBERS TO BUY THEIR OWN. DO NOT EVEN THINK OF PHOTOCOPYING PAGES AS THIS REPRESENTS THEFT OF INTELLECTUAL PROPERTY AND THESE CONTENTS ARE COPYRIGHTED. SUPPORT OUR ADVERTISERS WHO HELP MAKE KA'NU CULTURE POSSIBLE.
PLEASE FEEL FREE TO CONTRIBUTE STORIES, SUGGESTIONS AND QUALITY PHOTOGRAPHS TO OUR OFFICE DURING THE YEAR. WE'RE NOW ON THE INTERNET FOR ALL OF THOSE WHO PADDLE THE NET, SO EMAIL US SOMETIME.
PADDLE HARD, KEEP OUR OCEANS CLEAN . . . AND HAVE A NICE DAY!
THE MANAGEMENT OF BATINI BOOKS.

Walter Guild

Let me begin by saying that Walter Guild is no ordinary individual - as he would like to think of himself.

An outstanding athlete, a true gentleman and considered by many contemporaries as Mr Canoeing, it is not so much what Walter gets out of the sport, but more importantly what he puts in to it, which makes him a rare and special individual.

Walter's considerable contributions to the sport include instigating the design and production of the Hawaiian Class Racer (Classic) canoe during the early 1980's and later in 1994 the advancement of that design to the Force 5. The development of solo canoes from lagoon style to open ocean craft with the creation of the Kaiwi Challenger (Ocean Master in Australia) and the establishment of open ocean events to cater for solo divisions in Hawaii, including a solo Moloka'i race.

Beyond this, his contributions to the sport of outrigger canoe racing are many and varied. He has become a catalyst for much of what happens around the Pacific (and elsewhere) in terms of the development of outrigger canoe padding.

Of course he'll deny it, but that's the kind of guy he is. I couldn't help but feel dwarfed by not only his physical size of six foot something or other, but also his extensive knowledge of the sport. Inside Walter Guild's head there is clearly a veritable labyrinth of knowledge.

Since leaving college, Walter has made outrigger canoeing his life. It was then, in 1979, that he bought into the Fiberglass Shop which at the time was manufacturing fiberglass Malia canoes.

Since that time he has established Canoe Sports Hawaii with the primary objective of advancing the sport of outrigger canoe racing around the world particularly in the area of solo canoes and the events that can be created around them.

Parts of Walter Guild's interview are also included in the stories on solo canoes and ama.

1

Walter Guild's number plate speaks volumes about a man completely dedicated to outrigger canoeing. From building and designing, to paddling and coaching, outrigger canoe racing is his life. The sport is fueled by individuals such as this - motivated by a love of the sport and a desire to recycle energy back into it. Nurturing the sport toward better things; be it the betterment of equipment, techniques or events.

Could you talk about the Fiberglass Shop and what the function of Canoe Sports Hawaii is?

Essentially they are tied together. Canoe Sports Hawaii came about because I really didn't like the name Fiberglass Shop as a name for trying to sell Hawaiian canoes. Its a generic name that could be in Long Beach, California. Also the Fiberglass Shop represents more than just canoes because for many years we had made many other items from fiberglass.

We felt that as Hawaiian canoes were the one thing we manufactured and sold ourselves, it would be nice to have a marketing name with a logo which we could sell those under.

The other thing we started getting into was that we began designing new forms of canoes. We needed to create events by which these canoes could be used, thereby promoting them and generating sales. The solo canoes we manufacture are a perfect

example of that. We initiated the Kaiwi Channel crossing (Moloka'i) and other races whereby we created the event and then filled canoes with participants. Ultimately this division of the sport expanded so it has now become a market of its own. Canoe Sports Hawaii grew out of that.

When did you first become involved in outrigger canoeing?

I began paddling in 1970 in Thirteen and Under and steadily since then. I may have missed one or two years. I played football in college and became very large, so serious paddling was not something I was able to do. Instead I coached and paddled in four man crews during the summers, pretty much from 1970-80, through all the age divisions. After college I paddled my first Moloka'i race.

When we were kids we would do the long distance races through the Sixteen's, so we had quite a bit of experience by the time we paddled Moloka'i in the Men's division.

By 1980 we had a good young bunch of guys who stuck together and it was about as professional a crew as you could get. In that year, with some of the older guys, we won – first time out! And Outrigger went on to win for quite a few consecutive years. Out of the last fifteen years I've paddled Moloka'i twelve times.

You've had a long term relationship with the Outrigger Canoe Club of Hawaii . . .

Yes, my parents were members so I pretty much grew up at the club. My family goes way back with the club's history. My grandmother's brother was Walter MacFarlane, who died when he was president of the club in the 1940's. In honour of his memory, Outrigger stages its largest race (the July Fourth MacFarlane Regatta) which was established before the Moloka'i race.

So, yes, I'm very attached to the club and I grew up in the system, being exposed to it all. Right away I recognized that the canoes were something I wanted to be a part of. From being a sixteen year old kid working on the Koa canoes and being around helping with coaching, it rapidly became a part of my life.

I was president myself in 1994, and have coached a number of divisions. In 1981, I was head coach with assistance, and have coached periodically since, including the women for a couple of years. Most recently in 1993, I coached our upper division and in 1994 I had back surgery so I coached.

When did you first become involved with Fiberglass Shop?

1980, but the shop has been here since the sixties. Its primary function was in the manufacture of canoes; manufacturing the first production fiberglass outrigger canoes in Hawaii (the Malia class) which created an entire fleet. This helped get the sport really up and moving.

A couple of friends of mine, members of Outrigger, saw an ad in the paper in 1979 that the shop was for sale and became concerned knowing that this was the source of fiberglass outrigger canoes. So they put together a select group of people who purchased it to keep it going. When I got out of college, they asked me if I would be interested in running it, and I went for it. Over time, I have bought them all out, so that now I am the only one left.

At what stage did you feel the need to offer an alternative design to the Malia?

It really started to happen around 1976 when the Tahitians came out to Hawaii and won the Moloka'i in their own canoe. That began a big revolution. Out of this came the Hawaiian Canoe Racing Association (HCRA) specifications. Once they were established, people started building canoes that were fast but complied with these specifications. So a number of one-off's were made – no two canoes being alike, there were no moulds.

As we progressed into the eighties it became apparent that we needed a production manufactured canoe similar to what the Malia had been. One that everybody could have access to and which would be competitive with the one-off canoes.

So we contracted a fabulous designer by the name of Joe Quigg, surfboard designer and catamaran builder, who had a real interest in all of this. We built a couple of models to one-quarter scale and took them back to the Steven's Institute of Technology in New Jersey where we tank-tested them. We came up with a design that we felt was the best hull for both rough and calm water, for turning and holding a straight line, with all the best compromises in a hull design. We named it the Hawaiian Class Racer.

Joe shaped the plug out of foam. We built a one-off from that. Paddled it, tried it and it was a big hit – right off the bat! We took a mould from the plug and went into production. That canoe became, around the world, the standard production canoe for everyone, first available in 1982.

Where else are they made?

Only Hawaii and Australia. In 1983 at the time Australia won the America's Cup, Keith Williams and Max Christmas had been in Newport, Rhode Island. On their way home, they saw the Moloka'i race and said "You know what? That's our America's Cup. We want to win that race!"

So they approached the Outrigger Club which won the race that year, and said they wanted two people to come to Australia who would teach their athletes down there, and get the sport set up. One of the contact people was a good friend and past partner in the Fiberglass Shop, Hank Lass, an older gentleman and a real good paddler at the time. The other was myself, as I had been in the winning crew. We went to Australia in 1983 and spent a week in Surfers Paradise and a week on Hamilton.

Then in 1984, Keith brought out a crew

Walter's athleticism, lifetime dedication to outrigger paddling and continual analytic style, has meant that he has an understanding of the dynamics of the sport beyond those who simply paddle. He takes little at face value and is always looking for ways to squeeze the best out of every situation to maximize its potential, be it whilst paddling or in contemplating new designs. It is this motivation that makes him such an important figure in outrigger canoeing today. Photographed here paddling in Australia at the Hamilton Cup.

In 1989 Walter pioneered the first Moloka'i race across the Kaiwi Channel for solo canoes. Some people considered "Toots" Minvielle's idea of a race across the channel in six person canoes as madness. Paddling the channel on a flimsy solo craft however, at the beginning stages of its technological development from lagoon to open ocean, could be seen as perhaps an even greater act of madness! It nevertheless represents an historic and significant milestone in the development of the solo class in particular and outrigger canoe racing in general.

Only three solo canoes made the first crossing (two fewer than when the first six person canoe crossing was made in 1952). With further development, open ocean solo paddling has become a boom sport; growing more rapidly than either kayak or surf ski paddling - not just in Hawaii but far and wide from California to Australia.

Outrigger canoeing is now available to those who wish to go it alone in an open ocean environment - which for some is far more enticing than flat water paddling. The implications are enormous worldwide.

and we built them a Hawaiian Class Racer which they used in the Moloka'i race. They did very well their first year (third or fourth I think). They didn't think so. They thought they should have won. But it isn't the sort of race you turn up to for the first time and win. (*Unless you're Tahitian! - Ed.*) They took their canoe back to Hamilton Island and we licensed them for manufacture.

What other countries have you exported canoes to?

Throughout the whole of the Pacific region where outrigger canoe racing is practiced: Canada, Guam, Tahiti, Marshall Islands, Tonga, northern and southern California, and now Oregon – all around the Pacific.

What about the Malia class - do you still get orders for these?

We do periodically. We have not built many of them. The most widely used fleets of Malia are on the west coast (USA) – they still use them quite a bit. All regatta (sprints) racing must be in Malia canoes and they have a Malia class in all of their long distance races. We've built a few of them over the last couple of years and sent them to California. They tell me that they will be continuing to order Malia canoes because whilst their original fleet is getting older, they have decided to maintain that class.

That is good to hear because the Malia is a "classic" canoe in the real sense. It seems to resemble the old fishing canoes.

Exactly. They have a lot of character, turn well and pick up a big following sea pretty easily too. The Malia is an interesting boat if you've read anything about it. They were originally made from solid log.

The builder, Yamasaki, a Japanese boat-builder and woodworker, built three of them in Kona around 1933. All three are still in existence with two of them belonging to the Outrigger Canoe Club and still down there, *Leilani* and *Kakina*.

The other was owned by a member and very famous coach of the Outrigger Club, Dad Center (the women's long distance race is named after him). He sold it to the people who started the Waikiki Surf Club. They took the boat and pared it all out, making it into a really beautiful racing canoe at the time. It had a wonderful crew for years and years and won so many races that it was considered to be *the* canoe.

Around the early sixties the canoe was shipped to the west coast to paddle in the Catalina race. Prior to it being sent back some people in California made up a fiberglass mould and started producing fiberglass Malia canoes and moulds. The owners of the original were not too thrilled about it as they were not in on the deal. Then one of the fiberglass moulds from California was sold here in Hawaii and it was used for the existing moulds in Hawaii.

So originally, it was made on the mainland off the Koa original. By the time it got to be used for production here, it had been taken off the fiberglass.

How do we get the term "Classic"?

"Classic" became a slang or a nickname that people around the world came up with in shortening the name Hawaiian Class Racer. So many people use that name now that I even find myself calling it that too. The Hawaiian Class Racer has become the "Classic" through usage.

How many Hawaiian Class Racers have you made over the years?

Estimating that amount accurately is difficult – probably close to four hundred. It's quite an experience for me to walk down to the canoes at a big race like the Hamilton Cup and see the number of Hawaiian Class Racers in use. I wish that I had a royalty for each one like I was supposed to!

It's not a bad situation now that we've moved on designwise. In my opinion that

Photo Jason Somerville-Kimlin

The Malia Class represented the first mass produced fiberglass outrigger canoe. Three were originally shaped from Koa on the Kona coast of the Big Island of Hawaii, one of which found its way to California to participate in the Catalina race. A mould was made from that Koa canoe and the Malia Class was born. A mould was made in Hawaii at the Fiberglass Shop during the sixties and, in time, the popularity of the Malia formed the backbone of contemporary fiberglass manufactured outrigger canoes and canoe racing. Still used exclusively in Canada and during the regatta (sprint) season in California, this classic canoe in every sense, is still providing pleasure to a great number of paddlers.

hull has now become our gift to canoe racing and we're not concerned about it being reproduced because we're not going to have to face selling against that ourselves. Our original arrangement with Australia was that none of the canoes were to come out of there to compete directly on our market.

Let's talk about the Bradley canoe. First shaped by Hawaii's Sonny Bradley and manufactured in California for some time before coming to Hawaii, the Bradley canoe has, over six to eight years

Walter outside the Fiberglass Shop holding the one-quarter scale model of the Hawaiian Class Racer (Classic) which was one of two models made and tank tested. This model passed the test and so the Hawaiian Class Racer was born.

now become popular here. What impact did that canoe have on racing in this country and on the Hawaiian Class Racer?

The Bradley canoe had been in existence for a long time, parallel to the Hawaiian Class Racer. People in California began to like the Bradley canoe more and more and increasingly used it. They felt that it was faster in their conditions, but it was never really thought of as being something that would work better in Hawaii. A couple of Bradley boats came here about three or four years ago and did fairly well but the first ones here were not necessarily with very strong crews, so the perception was that.

Then better crews brought them over and came in the top three or four at Moloka'i – opening some eyes. What really did it was when Tahiti paddled one in 1993 and won Moloka'i going under five hours for the first time! Once that happened, then the Bradley was the hottest thing that everyone had to have. There is now a license holder in Hawaii who pays royalties. He can manufacture here but not sell outside Hawaii.

When did advances on the Hawaiian Class Racer start coming about?

One of the strong influences on that was the Tahitians. We had discussions with them and agreed that the "Classic" if it had a little more width through the centre and a little more rocker would be a very similar canoe to the Bradley and would probably perform with many of the same characteristics in rough water.

We had an opportunity to try in 1994 and made a prototype by taking a thin shell out of the mould, cutting it and adding material to it.

7

CANOE SPORTS
HAWAII

91-291 KALAELOA BLVD., B-5 • EWA BEACH, HAWAII 96707
808 • 682 • 5233 FAX : 808 • 682 • 1071

MANUFACTURERS AND SUPPLIERS OF
FORCE 5. 43'5" SIX PERSON CANOE
HAWAIIAN CLASS RACER. 43'4" SIX PERSON CANOE
MALIA. 40' SIX PERSON CANOE
HAWAIIAN 0-3 STILETTO. 30' FOUR PERSON TOURING CANOE
HAWAIIAN SURF CLASS 2200 SERIES. 22' SURFING CANOE
HAWAIIAN JUNIOR CLASS 1500 SERIES. 15' SURFING CANOE
KAIWI CHALLENGER. 23' SINGLE PERSON CANOE WITH RUDDER
CANOE TRAILERS

We had also been approached by a number of our steady customers who had bought boats from us over the years (who had been using them for ten or twelve years and some of those same canoes still in perfect condition). They mentioned that they liked our product and construction and vowed that if we could make something comparable to a Bradley that they would keep buying our canoes.

So we said to ourselves "Okay that's good enough." We didn't have to design something that was fifty percent percent better in order for people to buy our product. We were a bit conservative, used our heads and acknowledged that some of the design concepts on the Bradley work well, while at the same time trying to maintain as much of the Hawaiian Class Racer design as possible. That's how we went forward with the project.

The first thing that strikes you about the Force 5 is the increased rocker. How does this affect the steerer's ability to catch runners in a way that is different to the "Classic"?

Now one of the main differences between the Force 5 and the Bradley is that the ends of the Force 5 continue that rocker curve more. The Bradley has a certain amount of rocker through the centre and the ends are somewhat straighter than the Force 5. That was something that we liked designwise and wanted to maintain.

We had evaluated that one of the reasons the Bradley works so well in the open ocean is that its "footprint" on the water is more consistent. Working much like a rocking chair which, when it rocks, has the same amount of rocker in contact with the floor. In canoe terms, when it's in the trough or gets up to the top, its wetted

The Hawaiian Class Racer ("Classic") was developed as a result of the Tahitians using their own design during the 1976 Moloka'i race and thrashing all other canoes in that event. The Hawaiian Canoe Specifications were then drawn up to standardize design elements. Some one-off canoes were made for a time, but there was a need to produce a fast fiberglass canoe that fitted in with the required specifications and could carry on where the Malia had left off - a canoe available to everyone.

surface area remains more consistent.

As opposed to a longer, straighter hull which when in a trough has its ends underwater and a water line extending the full length of the canoe, then at the top of a swell your water line length decreases drastically. These continual shifts in water line and wetted surface area are changes of drag on the hull – and therefore changes of speed. So the more you can reduce this lengthening and shortening of water line

The queen! The foam plug shaped by Joe Quigg from which a mould was made and all subsequent Hawaiian Class Racers have been born in one form or another.

Suspended here at Walter's factory is the perfect exhibit for an outrigger canoe museum. This was truly the very first Hawaiian Class Racer to size - which now has found its way all around the Pacific.

length, the more constant hull speed you will have. This is what you want to achieve.

The crew then is not coming off and on the power - upsetting rhythm and momentum?

Absolutely. The primary gain is in constant hull speed. A lot of lift in the centre of the boat as its accelerates so that it surfs well.

The downside (to both the Bradley and the Force 5) is that they are tough boats to steer. The steerer is now higher up out of the water and has a harder time finding solid water. Because the ends of the canoe are in the air more, it can pivot on its centre more readily – which is what it wants to do. The steerer becomes even more of a factor in these than in the Classic or Malia.

If you don't have an experienced steerer in rough water then you might be better off taking a Classic?

Many people are beginning to realize this now. You may come here with an all-world crew that can really make a Bradley or a Force 5 hull sing, but if the steerer can't keep it on line and keeps getting knocked sideways, killing the hull speed, your average hull speed over the length of that race may well be higher in a Classic where you can maintain speed. Your top hull speed capability may not be as high, but your *average* is better – which many paddlers overlook. In long open ocean races such as the Moloka'i it is the higher averages that will win.

Let's put a Force 5 up against a Classic in flat water and race them off, how do you think they would compare?

All the design criteria indicate that the Classic ought to be faster. Strangely enough I don't know if that's the case. We haven't as yet had a lot of experience with the canoe in flat water but it would really be a toss up at this point. The Classic should be a little bit quicker on the flat.

By all accounts the Force 5 is proving very popular and the Fiberglass Shop is working hard to keep up with orders. I heard that Tom Connor's decision to order one on behalf of the Tahitian crew was something of a catalyst for increased orders - much like when they used a Bradley in 1993.

Yeah. Well the Tahitians are considered by many to be state of the art in terms of canoe paddling. They've been going fast and the paddling community looks to them for new developments.

Tom is very well respected in terms of technical skills and evaluation. I have had conversations with him where he has told me he really likes the Force 5. In Hawaii, the Tahitians have both a Bradley and a Force 5. I'm anticipating that when they come to town they are going to paddle in both and the crew will then compare them.

From Tom's point of view and from his feedback, he seems to like the Force 5. One of the things it does a little better than the Bradley is tracking a bit more. It has a little of the "Classic" characteristic that in a sea, you can point it in a direction and it will tend to hold the line a little better – so the steerer is not having to work quite as hard.

We wanted to get that out of the design as we wanted to cater for women paddlers also. The Bradley is a big boat for women – very difficult for a female steerer in rough water. We were hoping we could reach a compromise that would allow some of the characteristics of the "Classic" to remain in the Force 5. By accounts, that is there.

> **The Tahitians are considered by many to be state of the art in terms of canoe paddling.**

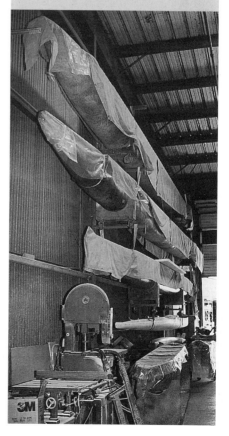

From the top and under wraps. The original Hawaiian Class Racer mould, the Malia mould, a mould for the Stiletto (a thirty foot sailing canoe hull) and below that, the Kaiwi Challenger solo canoe that changed the face of solo outrigger paddling from lagoon to open ocean.

An historical smorgasbord representing the birthplace of so many canoes.

The Hawaiian Class Racer above, basically without rocker (curvature) throughout its length except at the extremities, though still a fine ocean craft has somewhat less surfing ability than a canoe with substantially more rocker fore and aft. It is, however, more forgiving, possibly quicker on the flat and easier to steer. Don't right it off by any means!

The Force 5 canoe has increased rocker allowing it to fit into swells more efficiently and therefore picking up runners better. It has a more consistent wetted surface area, keeping hull speed more consistent in the ocean. The Force 5 is more demanding of the steerer in open ocean conditions.

The Bradley is about a foot longer as well as being wider and deeper. Is this why a heavier crew (like this year's Lanikai men) favour it?

This seems to be unanimous at this stage. All the women's teams so far have preferred the Force 5.

The little cut out of the manu, clearly isn't there to make the canoe go

faster. How did it come about?

That is purely Brent Bixler here in the factory – one hundred percent. I walked past one day and he had taken a saw and just attacked the manu. I said "What is that?" He wanted a bit of creative license – to put something in there so we don't just have another canoe. We left it and I like it!

The potential was that this would

The Bradley Canoe, designed and shaped by Hawaiian Sonny Bradley, was the first production made six-person outrigger canoe that had added rocker (curvature) throughout its hull length - in order to increase its ability to catch and surf swell or wind chop. First made popular and manufactured in California, the Bradley canoe certainly performed well in the relatively calm waters there, before it came to be manufactured in Hawaii.

Sonny is an accomplished Koa canoe builder whose thirst for knowledge about canoe construction has led him to observe the techniques and traditions of Tahitians and North American Indians as well as those of Hawaii. Like Walter, Sonny's contribution to outrigger canoeing makes him an important and central figure in its development. His creation of the Bradley has been the catalyst for a new generation of six-person outrigger canoes that will serve to increase our enjoyment as canoes perform to ever better standards in the open ocean environment.

become a recognizable trade mark of the Force 5 – and it has. Paddlers will look for that cut as canoes go by on a trailer, or in the ocean, and they can identify the Force 5 by it, straight away.

What prompted you to support the idea of having a Canoe Sports Australia?

Well Australia has become a unique place. It is a tremendous growth area. and obviously the people there have accepted the sport and taken it up with a huge amount of energy and vitality. With regard to competition, Australia is a world leader. As one of the four main regions – Australia, Tahiti, Hawaii and California – Australia is at the top of that heap. Very much so.

Yet it is somewhat more isolated than the other three regions. California and Hawaii are USA while Tahiti has its own history and cultural links with the canoes. Australia needs to have access to a certain amount of that, yet will have to stand alone and grow from within.

It became clear that in order for us, not only Canoe Sports Hawaii but also Hawaiians, to remain an influence and give direction there (versus going completely on their own coming up with new designs, or having Tahiti, or someplace else, become their connection) we would have to become actively involved in supplying Australians with what we know and have learned.

I anticipate that the gap, even though we have years on them, is closing fast. Training techniques, paddles and many other things are already beginning to come the other direction. People here are waiting to see what the Australians are going to come up with.

In Hawaii we still have the biggest race. The conditions we experience are unique and we have the opportunity to develop within those conditions. So we become the test-tank in many respects. As of right now, we can develop suitable products and we have worked very hard to establish a name and identity which just became a natural

Ready for delivery. On the tarmac, a new Force 5 and cradled above, two Hawaiian Class Racers destined for a junior development program. Note the difference in rocker, in manu shape and also a slight bulge in the mid-section.

with the people involved. I had not gone out and sought somebody to take our name down there. It is a long distance away and hard to keep track of things – so they had to be the right people.

Just to round off, what are your impressions of the way outrigger canoeing is developing ?

I think outrigger canoe racing is the next explosion sport. Similar to surfing and windsurfing which became the real "in-thing" to be doing. Although we have seen it coming for some time, I think we have underestimated the speed at which it would come about.

I think with the development of solo, lighter weight, high performance canoes, and an attraction at all levels spreading world-wide, that the next big explosion point is Europe – where, in fact, it has already begun.

There was a team from Hungary this year at the Moloka'i race. Swedish women have paddled with Offshore California and Swedish men have also made contact. We have sent two of the smaller surfing canoes to France. So Europe seems to me to be the next real explosion point.

We are also in the process of setting up a similar situation as with Australia, on the east coast of the United States. It is also too remote for Canoe Sports Hawaii to service from here – as it includes the Caribbean, the Florida Coast and way up the east coast. I'm dealing with somebody from New York, but we will see where it finally sets up.

On behalf of many paddlers thanks for your dedication to the sport.

I think outrigger canoe racing is the next big explosion sport. Similar to surfing and windsurfing which became the real "in thing" to be doing. The next big explosion point is Europe, where, in fact, it has already begun.

Two similar angles – above a Bradley canoe at the Catalina race and below a Force 5 in the Skippy race, Oahu.

The Bradley is a bigger canoe in every way. A foot longer thereabouts, as well as wider and deeper, it has been very successful and is suited especially well to physically larger and heavier crews.

The Force 5, whilst still able to accommodate heavy crews, is more popular with female crews. It is already beginning to enjoy a string of wins in its home waters of Hawaii, in all divisions.

Know Your Manu...

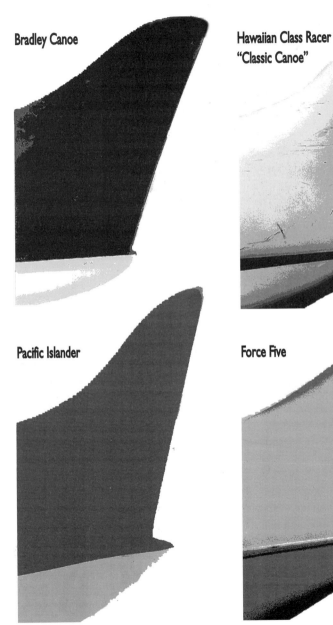

Bradley Canoe

**Hawaiian Class Racer
"Classic Canoe"**

Pacific Islander

Force Five

J first started making paddles for myself and close friends from a corner section of the back yard shed. Over time, the shed became a state of the art fully temperature controlled workshop with baking oven and Pirie Paddles was formed in 1987.

Right from the beginning J pioneered the use of epoxy resins on timber paddles. The super strength of epoxy enables me to use lightweight fiberglass cloth over the blade area giving the paddle a strong, non-flexing face which doesn't slide off the stroke. A two pack epoxy finish gives the paddle a mirror surface and protects against impact.

Jn my early paddles J used a lot of Balsa, but found that it damaged easily and drew water. So now J don't use any, but choose from clear Cedar, White Wood, Kavula and solid Spruce for the shafts. Always aiming for that perfect blend of strength and lightness.

As people have experimented with paddle design, J have made paddles of many different shapes and sizes. Each club seemed to have its own particular preference – J have made some paddles so large that a small child could not pick them up! And some so small that they would require a stroke rate of eighty a minute!

Over the last couple of years things have moved away from these radical extremes with an optimum size emerging of approximately eighteen to nineteen inches in blade length, fuller shoulder and a little over nine inches across the blade.

Orders for blade faces over the years have also varied greatly. Some with a big scoop on the face or a dihedral running down the middle. However, disturbance created at the front causes cavitation at the back and the paddle will not grab the water well, fluttering through the pull. Not good for the technique because paddling involves planting the blade cleanly and then pulling the canoe past the paddle. Any cavitation or disturbance around the blade causing loss of grip on the water will reduce your effectiveness as a paddler.

J have done a lot of R&D on blade shape and have a lot of input from people involved with the sport. My paddles first crossed the Kaiwi Channel in the Moloka'i event in 1990 when J was in the Surfers Paradise crew with Trevor Hendy (current World Jron Champion) Dwayne Thuys (former World Jron Champion) and Jan "Lats" Rowlings (1992 Barcelona K4 bronze).

With the help of these guys and in particular "Lats", we have produced a most advanced carbon fibre outrigger paddle which is a single piece design with no weak points and feels like a timber paddle through the water. The face has a smooth kick at the bottom and a rounded dihedral with a clean, fine reinforced edge

In the earliest record of tattooeing it was found that the Pacific Islanders used to tatoo themselves with turtles and canoe paddles. The shell is a symbol of strength. Clumsy on land the turtle is a fast hydrodynamically efficient creature underwater. A Zig Zag pattern represents the ocean in Polynesian tatoo designs. "Inspired by nature, mastered by science".

giving it a knife like action on entry. Just what you need for excellent catch and clean exit.

We call this the Pirie Carbon Paddle. Each paddle is laid up in a pre-heated mould and then placed in a baking oven to post cure. This process increases the strength of the epoxy by up to thirty or forty percent. The shaft and head are one piece for added strength and the epoxy finish provides a high gloss, low friction surface which doesn't cause blistered hands. These paddles are AOCRA approved and cost only marginally more than timber – but should last up to three years longer. We will lend you a demo paddle too.

The mould for the Pirie Carbon Paddle is also being used to make fibreglass training paddles for beginning outrigger canoe paddlers as these can take a lot more abuse than the timber paddles.

I look forward to hearing from you with any inquiries. For contact details see my ad in this book. For the south Pacific and Micronesia, please contact Rod McLaughlin at Ocean Technologies.

Rob Pirie in his purpose built curing room inspects the progress of one of his paddlles.

A Sport on the Edge - Walter J Guild

PRESIDENT CANOE SPORTS HAWAII, THE FIBERGLASS SHOP AND RACE DIRECTOR OF THE KAIWI CHALLENGE.

Solo outrigger canoe paddling has become the fastest growing water sport in Hawaii. We have seen a four-fold increase in the past two years and have surpassed the surf ski in total participant numbers. Entry level into single person paddling craft has made a giant shift towards the solo canoe due to its short learning curve and overall stability. Weight and size have now become a factor that adds to the attraction of the canoes and continues to interest new and experienced paddlers alike.

A primary factor in the recent jump in participation has been the introduction of shorter, lighter hulls that perform better in open seas and are easier to transport and store. During the first years of open ocean solo paddling, the design and weight of the hulls limited the appeal of the sport to primarily large, strong males who could "horse" the canoes around both on land and in the water. Although determining the optimum design can be disputed, it would be easy to agree that the ideal length for all-round conditions is between twenty-one and twenty-three feet. A slightly shorter, wider boat with somewhat more bottom rocker, allows for superior handling in everything but the smoothest of conditions.

As participation and competitiveness has grown in Hawaii, so has advancement in design construction techniques. While restrictions on the hull design have been eliminated, a minimum weight for the biggest race with international competition, The Kaiwi Challenge, has been maintained. The reason for a minimum weight in this one race is to ensure that everyone has a competitive piece of equipment – not just those who can afford to spend the most money.

I am a firm believer in standardization of the larger six-person club-owned canoes, and in the early years I had concerns regarding hull weight and design of the solo canoes, however, it has become a great asset to solo design, to be allowed more leeway. I would be willing to bet that the sport will make a significant jump in participation and interest because of this.

We have spurred a new industry around this sport with a number of manufacturers all producing to capacity. Safety has also been a consideration, even though the latest group of light, stiff canoes has become the finest made; as modern technology is attracted to the manufacturing process.

1995 has shown us the full potential of solo paddling. Participant numbers for racing are close to one hundred with many times that number using canoes for recreation. The top solo paddlers have become recognized and respected sports heroes with coverage of certain events on local television.

The past two years have proved to be the most exciting and fulfiling for all those involved in our area of the sport. Every paddler will be truly amazed at what these little canoes are capable of achieving in terms of speed, excitement and participation.

Solo Explosion!

Six-person outrigger canoe racing has astounded many with its amazing popularity and continued growth throughout the Pacific and Pacific Rim countries. Well, hold onto your backsides, because there is a second wave, with the sudden overwhelming attraction to a craft that has been around in one form or another for thousands of years – the solo outrigger canoe.

Put simply, this craft is the ultimate individual outrigger paddling freedom beast. Suited to free-spirited individuals who revel in the challenge of individual accomplishment and freedom from constraint in an ocean environment.

Solo outrigger canoe racing as a sport in its own right has begun to contribute enormously to the growth of outrigger canoe racing, attracting paddlers from other paddle-sport disciplines and appealing to those who find it better suits their lifestyle or personality.

Solo outrigger canoe paddling is hardly a new concept in ocean craft. However its appeal was only ever going to be limited by design constraints and any related restrictions as to the paddling environment.

The Tahitians have raced solo in lagoon type environments for many years. Yet, despite having no limiting design specifications as such, the concept of constructing them into something more than a flat water craft seemed to be overlooked.

Their solo canoes are often of extremely light construction – either thin laminated woods with fiberglass coverings, or hi-tech models constructed with exotic materials. Rubber lashings are often incorporated as part of their design for simplicity and greater flexibility.

Construction materials aside, the basic design principles largely catered for flat water paddling. Such canoes were open decked so as in rough water they fill and are therefore unsuitable for open ocean

Walter Guild and Brent Bixler designed the Kaiwi Challenger so as to advance solo paddling from flat water lagoon restrictions to the excitement and challenge of the open ocean. Consequently, open ocean solo paddling has flourished in Hawaii. It has had instant appeal to many outrigger paddlers, as well as those from other paddle sport disciplines, who can now practice, race and improve their outrigger canoe paddling skills alone, without being restricted to protected waters or by the schedules of others.

Walter here paddling in Australia on the first of the production made Kaiwi Challenger by Canoe Sports Australia, re-named the Ocean Master for the Australian market.

paddling. *The lack of a rudder makes very great demands on the paddler to be an expert who must be fit, strong and perhaps have an even greater degree of ocean sense and knowledge in order to handle such craft in open water.*

By rethinking the fundamental design elements of a lagoon style solo outrigger canoe and focusing on transforming it into an open ocean craft, two relatively easy modifications had to be made almost without hesitation – a closed-in deck and a foot peddle operated rudder.

In this respect we already have a great deal of knowledge thanks to surf ski technology and to a lesser degree sea kayak design, being a sit inside deal rather than a sit on top.

But of course nothing is that simple. You need more than a closed deck and a rudder to make a miraculous transformation from lagoon paddling to the rigors of the open ocean. What was needed was a rigid, rugged construction that could guarantee no leaks and no unstable seams to separate.

A flat bottom suitable to flat water was not going to work either. More rocker had to be added and consideration given to the volume in the front section to prevent nose-diving. The rigging had to be beefed up and an ama created to suit the purpose. **Walter Guild of Canoe Sports Hawaii briefly explains the process.**

"I wonder: what if we did this, so as we could do that?"
The kind of thinking which developed the sport
of solo, open ocean, outrigger canoes.

Solo canoes seem to be a strong part of Canoe Sports Hawaii?

Absolutely. One of the reasons is that we feel that Canoe Sports Hawaii started open ocean paddling with rudders and other developments. This was definitely our big contribution. We took the boat from the 1986 Sprint Championships – an open decked, lagoon style Tahitian canoe – then we put a deck on it and a rudder. Then started paddling out in the open ocean racing and promoting them.

It was simply down to "I wonder what if we did this, so as we could do that?" kinda thinking that developed the sport of solo, open ocean canoeing. Those canoes were still essentially lagoon canoes. They were far from perfect. So we developed the Kaiwi Challenger – purpose built. Not egotistically speaking, the sport originated with Canoe Sports Hawaii.

Brent Bixler had a lot to do with the design of the Kaiwi Challenger (Ocean Master in Australia).

He and I both worked on the Force 5 and the Kaiwi Challenger. He was the hands-on component of these designs. My input comes purely from the water to the shop, whilst Brent's input comes from the material, the moulding and the shaping to the finished product.

So you give Brent the feedback about what you want to achieve ?

Yeah, I'll tell him what I want to achieve and what I think will work – you know: "a little wider in the back" or "I'd like to see a bow this way." Especially with the Kaiwi Challenger: I had envisaged what we needed to get out of it. We did full-size drawings, adding and taking away, then he shaped it. Just like we did with the Force 5.

When did the Kaiwi Channel race begin?

1989 was its first year and it was done with only three canoes, all identical. We wanted to try the concept of two people per canoe with changes. I felt that the course from the Kaluakoi hotel on Moloka'i to Waikiki, which was not used by anybody, would be the best option. The Moloka'i event is from Laau to Waikiki and the kayak race goes to Hawaii Kai both of which go across the wind a lot more. This course is more down wind and therefore a better surfing race.

The first year we tried it, it worked really well. The following year we had

Solo outrigger canoe paddling is here to stay. Having the potential to appeal to a huge cross section of people: of all ages, from all walks of life, from all around the globe. With inherent qualities of individualism, transportability and stability it is an ideal candidate to be the next global boom sport.

twelve canoes and it has pretty much doubled each year since. And now we have as many as fifty or sixty entrants.

Is there a wahini (women's) division?

Yes, and we have Open Men, Masters and Fifty and Over Masters. For the women it's quite a challenge and many didn't have the confidence to be out there in the Moloka'i Channel with just two of them. If something was to happen to one of them, the remaining paddler really has to take a big load. Many would not want to be the one who lets the other down.

So we opened it up and it can be either two or three paddlers – they can choose – still racing against each other in the same division. The thinking behind this was that two good women could sometimes be faster than three because if one of those isn't as strong, when she is paddling it's going to be slower. That is how it has kinda worked out; allowing a lot more teams to enter.

To what degree has this event helped the sport to create media interest and expansion throughout the islands?

It's helped tremendously. Previous to 1989 there were very few races – no kind of circuit. The kayaks were racing in their association during their season and solo outriggers weren't included at that stage.

After a few years of staging the Kaiwi Challenge and paddling the long boat canoes (twenty seven foot) which were quite a bit slower than kayaks and surf skis, designs improved. Weights and lengths reduced over time, so that pretty soon the solo outrigger canoes weren't much slower.

Are you getting a crossover from surf skis and kayaks to the solo's?

The growth now is in the solo division, not in surf skis or kayaks. Many of the top surf ski paddlers have crossed over, now paddling exclusively solo. Many were paddling surf skis as it was a good complement to their six-person canoe training. Well now, it is considered that the best complement to six-person training is of course the solo outrigger.

Many beginners now start solo as they can jump right on and be successful, whereas a surf ski takes quite a while before you can take it safely on the open ocean. As a result, the popularity of solo outrigger canoes has expanded.

The local association, Kanaka i Kaika, has now included solo canoes as equal partner in all of the racing. So we have racing that starts in November and continues through until May.

How many races would they stage over this time frame?

Approximately ten. We put on about four Canoe Sports Hawaii events. The first of the season held by us in November, called the King Kaulakaua Cup at Waikiki which includes solo's, surf skis, paddle boards and six-person canoes.

Then we stage a couple of smaller middle of season events which are ideally down wind surfing races. A couple of weeks before the big Moloka'i race, we put on a relay race for two paddlers over in Kailua which is a dress rehearsal for the Kaiwi Challenge.

This race is fantastic. The first person

Early morning, ripples and glints reflecting onto hulls bringing a sense of peace and calm before the race. With the popularity of this new paddle sport we are seeing a proliferation of new open ocean designs. "The Arrow" canoe (centre) built by Karel's Fiberglass Shop in Kailua, Oahu, is very much a rough water craft. Note the similarity in design to an Eskimo kayak bow: lots of volume, rocker and knife-like lines for splicing oncoming waves. We are seeing what are essentially hybrids or *bitsa* canoes – bits of this, bits of that – all part of the process of development.

Transportability has huge implications.
Solo outrigger canoes on roof racks and the open road in ever greater numbers. Enabling
paddlers to travel all over, taking their favourite paddle-craft with them. Spreading interest
in obscure places by their mere presence. Places, where previously an outrigger canoe of
any description, may never have been seen. Be it river, lake, dam, canal or open ocean.
Firsts will be created all over the planet.
Think of it – the first solo outrigger canoe to cross the English Channel,
the first to paddle the River Nile . . .

goes out into the bay at Kailua and comes into Lanikai, whilst the partner drives to meet them. They switch, then the second person goes out around the islands and down to Rabbit Island. The first paddler drives to this point and again changes, then paddles around Makapuu Head to Hawaii Kai, when an exciting switch is made by a paddler leaping off the rocks. The finish line is at the Outrigger Canoe Club, Diamond Head.

It is four stages, approximately equal in length, about an hour each, with land-based changes. The crowd watching moves to each change point, which makes for a great spectator sport as opposed to a normal long distance race.

Just as bodyboarding took the world by storm as an easy way to become involved with waveriding, offering a less threatening learning curve than stand-up surfing, so too, the solo outrigger canoe offers a relatively stable platform from which to begin venturing into the open ocean.

As equipment improves along with technique, so too the thrill factor will get turned up a notch or two as things that once were not possible, become a reality.

Sea kayak paddling requires a high degree of skill related to capsize dangers due to their nature of construction. Eskimo kayak paddlers were trained from childhood how to deal with a (life threatening) capsize – hence the Eskimo roll. Due to the frigid waters they

lived around, they would often sew their anoraks directly to the covers of the kayak. The only means of survival was therefore to roll back over.

The kayak is a fantastic paddle-craft and in no way can it be seen as anything less than the outrigger canoe. However its basic design assumption is that of a cold water craft offering protection from the elements. They are ideally suited to certain environments and

Flying the ama has become the most significant development in solo paddling technique in recent times and one which demands a lot of practice. It is a move used whilst on a runner in order to take advantage of ocean energy. To increase speed and maneuverability the ama is deliberately raised free of the water using the paddle blade on the offside as a brace by bouncing it across the water surface. This requires ocean knowledge and confidence in yourself and your gear. Only practice will give you that.

This particular technique is not completely unique to solo outrigger canoes. Surf ski paddlers often perform a similar technique in order to move across a wave face from left to right. It works by reducing the wetted surface area of the hull, increasing water line length, reducing drag – thus increasing hull speed.

Surf ski paddlers too, use the paddle as a brace by applying a degree of downwards pressure on the blade and the surface of the water. This prevents capsize as well as keeping your butt firm in the seat. Then the skill lies in working the foot peddles to stay on the wave.

Time on the water, experimentation and the desire to push equipment (and yourself) to the limit is central to the embryonic stage of anything. A blending of our physical and creative abilities with the potentials of the equipment we have access to, will always tend to reach a zenith. A point where either you as an individual cannot progress any further or the equipment you have has reached its maximum potential through your demands. It is from this that new levels of advancement in equipment emanate and so too, in skill and ability.

What of the future? Asymmetrical solo canoes for particular wave and swell conditions? A quiver of paddles, ama and iako? We have only just begun . . .

do require a reasonably high level of skill, not so much in paddling but in recovery after capsize.

This level of safety is emphasized in kayak schools across the world. Their primary concern is teaching capsize recovery techniques and safety.

Surf ski's of course offer the same freedom from fear of entrapment and being disabled by swamping as solo outrigger canoes do. Surf ski's are none-the-less quite unstable and require a high degree of balance skill to master in anything but flat water. One of their greatest attributes is that they are designed for surf use.

In its simplest form the surf ski can be likened to a warm water adaption of the sea kayak, being a sit on top deal. It is this which makes it theoretically more unstable as the paddler's centre of gravity is raised – unlike in a sea kayak where the paddler's centre of gravity is as low as it possibly can be thereby increasing stability.

It is possible that the wide use of sea kayaks, whilst remaining popular in temperate climates for adventure style paddling and

For kane (man) or wahine (woman), the solo outrigger canoe has great appeal. Don't think for one minute that they only appeal to those who already paddle six-person. The reality is that there is a huge pool of potential participants from other solo paddle-sports, such as kayaking and open canoeing, who have and will bypass the six-person facet of outrigger canoe racing to participate as specialist solo paddlers. A sport on the verge of big things.

Paddling with friends for fun and practice or against them in competition, solo outrigger canoe paddling offers many freedoms. One of its great benefits is that it allows six-person canoe paddlers to practice during the off season or at training times to suit individual schedules. Many will become specialist solo outrigger paddlers, others will balance both - paddling and racing outrigger canoes for practically the whole year round.

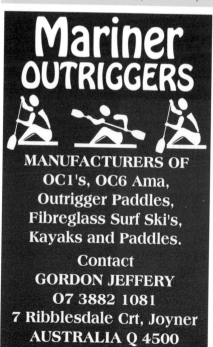
general recreational use, could ultimately be under some threat by recent developments in solo outriggers.

Even in cold to temperate conditions, with the way wet/dry suit technology has progressed since the sailboard epidemic of the 1980's, there is already a reduced need for an enclosed cockpit, as it were.

The implications are enormous. For example, we might consider why it is necessary to put beginners at a greater degree of risk learning kayaking when they could gain all the same benefits and similar skills through paddling the more stable solo outrigger canoes?

Variations in design have only just begun, and no doubt, a variety of models for specific purposes will appear – for touring, with deck webbings and storage compartments, or glass-bottomed for coral viewing. Manufacturers should have a fat time!

Setting yourself up on a wave, a swell or a runner (as the esoteric outrigger-speak goes) is essentially what downhill paddling is all about. Reducing paddling time and increasing gliding time! Letting the ocean provide the energy, whilst working in harmony with it for that extra speed.

Once up and gliding, your body weight is transferred to the off-side with your paddle outstretched over the water and bounced across it to maintain that fine line between balance and capsize.

The canoe quickly gains speed as resistance is reduced with the hull becoming more responsive to pressure on the foot peddles and shifts in body weight without drag on the ama. Cut backs and re-entries become a real part of staying on the wave.

Mens solo outrigger race – Kona Coast Hawaii. Te Biere went off and stayed that way until race end at Kailua-Kona. Fully committed to every stroke and nuance of the ocean.

Late Developments

With preparations under way for the 1996 solo outrigger canoe season in Hawaii, beginning in earnest in January, manufacturers and paddlers alike have been researching and developing to get just that bit more in terms of performance.

One thing which has been evident is the demand for a moulded seat of some type. With this the paddler can have increased lumbar support, better feel for the craft, more control over its movements especially when flying the ama – to feel more secure when leaning away from the ama. A firmer feel in the seat allows for more relaxed paddling and better energy transfer from paddle, to butt, to canoe.

Curiously enough, one would have thought that a moulded seat should have been *bleedin' obvious* (as the English would say). Moulded seats are nothing new in solo outrigger canoes in New Zealand for example, and have of course been standard on kayaks and surf skis forever.

However, manufacturers have now gone about moulding the seats in two different ways. Hawaii's Tom Connor has opted for the moulded recessed seat giving an overall appearance more like a surf ski.

Recessing the seat in this way has two effects – one good and one not so good. By lowering the paddler's centre of gravity, the canoe is in effect more stable. However being lower means that biomechanically, it is harder to exert as much pull or downwards thrust on the blade; so there could be a possible power deficit. A kayak paddle works efficiently with this seating arrangement as the path of the paddle is more out to the side as opposed to the single blade which follows a path more parallel to the canoe.

The seat in addition, custom-made to suit the owner's physical dimensions, will affect resale of the canoe in as much as finding a secondhand buyer near the exact height of the original owner reduces the number of potential buyers. Finding a partner for change over races of equal height may also present a problem.

So the best solution would seem to be an adjustable moulded seat. This is the path which Karel Tresnak of Karel's Fiberglass Products has taken. Although yet to have its first season, the concept seems sound; offering full adjustability and maintaining the paddler's ability to exert maximum pressure on a

Deck plan of Tom Connor's solo outrigger canoe. Surf ski refinements with recessed moulded seat. Note also the support for iako which is lashed on with rubber.

Tom Connor's solo outrigger canoe has most of the attributes of a surf ski. With moulded recessed seat and individual foot wells, the feet and seat are at the same height – fine for double blade kayak paddling but is it OK for single blade paddling? New designs, new ideas many of which are yet to have a full season.

traditional outrigger paddle.

In an effort to minimize water collection in recessed areas such as the footwells, some manufacturers have moved away from one large open well to smaller individual wells for the feet. One good thing about this also is that you no longer have the problem of knees pressing against the sides of a cowling.

The New Zealand designed Surfrigger from Moana Nui is a very neat set up. The paddler sits inside a recess much like a kayak, wearing a neoprene skirt to prevent water entering. (This design is popular in Tahiti, a sit inside deal with a skirt to prevent water entering).

Escape looks easy in the case of a huli, however I suspect that it would fill with water,

unlike the sit-on-top models, which do not take any water. The Surfrigger also has a foot operated bilge pump to keep the inside dry.

Meanwhile in Australia where aquatic creativity runs wild, one individual (who shall be known as *Fleety)* felt that because of the solo outrigger canoe's poor turning radius and general responsiveness related to a long water line length and the hindrance of the ama, he would use the principle applied to double-surf skis of rudders both fore and aft. This really is a slap in the face of tradition. Not so long ago it was no rudder. Then one – which ruffled the feathers of some traditionalists. Now, two!

The bottom line is that two does seem to work, making it more responsive to turn. However the system is possibly not without

John Martin's Honukai *(turtle)* canoe, is short (20'), lightweight and highly maneuverable. Notice plenty of volume up front and rocker throughout the length. Shortness definitely has benefits in the open ocean but not so on flat water. This model like many others is still having refinements added to it.

Karel Tresnak's Arrow built in Kailua Oahu. Kayak lines.

Australian manufactured Argonaut solo canoes are based on a hull plan which underwent much scientific testing to arrive at the eventual hull shape.

shorter. The outrigger assembly itself will no doubt come under modification, especially ama design, iako shape and materials. The latter seem to be moving away from timber in favour of alloy or graphite. Lightness and strength remains the issue.

John Martin's Honukai *(turtle)* canoes in Hawaii remain one of the shortest on the market at twenty feet by just under seventeen inches wide weighing forty-three pounds fully rigged. They are highly maneuverable and certainly have this as an advantage over longer canoes. Karel's Arrow canoes are also a small canoe with lots of rocker and many of the characteristics of sea kayaks.

It is not my intention to give a product review as such but rather to point out the varieties of approach. In conclusion, the following is a guideline to the type of characteristics being constructed today around the Pacific.

its drawbacks. Certainly increased drag is a problem. You also have to wonder how it would handle at high speed in the rough. Double surf ski paddlers have found some problems with two rudders as the ski tends to round up caused by high and low pressure areas building up on the rudder leading to cavitation. Sometimes also a fin can break free. Having said this, and depending on what the rules will allow, it has some positive aspects that should not be overlooked.

Canoes continue to get lighter, but not

* *Weights and lengths are subject to individual country's limits. These represent rough guides only. Development of solo outrigger designs are very much in a dynamic stage at present.*

LAGOON CANOES

Reflecting the traditional solo outrigger canoe designs of Tahiti, with flat rocker line, low freeboard, open deck, long water line length and an overall length of up to twenty seven feet, no rudder. Often extremely light weight, but generally around ten kilograms constructed of wood veneer and epoxy/kevlar (in Tahiti) or GRP. Minimum volume at extremities, maximum beam and volume in the mid-section. Feet below seat level which is often just a flat wooden block across the gunwales. Iako made from wood.

LAGOON/COASTAL CANOES

Subtle amount of rocker primarily in the forward section ahead of the seat. Enclosed deck, open foot well area in which both feet fit below the level of the seat, marginally higher freeboard, overall length of between twenty-four and twenty-six feet, rudder fitted sometimes detachable. Tending to be of GRP construction from about fifteen kilograms Increased volume overall, maximum being just forward of the footwells. Iako made from alloy or laminated timber.

OPEN OCEAN CANOES

Noticeable rocker extending fore and aft in varying amounts, higher freeboard, (but not in the case of a surfski style canoe), separate footwells minimize pooling, seat sometimes at same height as the foot wells. Length varies between twenty and twenty-four feet with a minimum weight around twelve kilograms when exotic cloths and resins are used. Maximum volume is further forwards in the bow. Iako mainly from alloy or carbon graphite. Sometimes moulded seats are added.

*"The traditional solo outrigger canoe
that's got you covered for all conditions"*

Canadian champion paddler Heather Taylor, paddling in the Queen Liliuokalani solo race Kailua-Kona Hawaii.

Heather hails from a background of flat water kayaking, war canoes, ocean kayaking, marathon canoeing, dragon boat racing and outrigger canoeing.

Cross over from other paddle-sport disciplines to solo outrigger canoe paddling will inevitably gather momentum as international participation increases and the word spreads.

Heather is a good example of someone who will have a go at any paddle sport, simply for the challenge and the love of most all paddle-sport disciplines.

You won't see much better technique than this. Maximum reach; locked elbows; torso rotation; blade entry close to the hull and running parallel; head still, looking forward, focused; relaxed recovery phase, with relaxed wrists and blade feathered.

Solo, Open Ocean Racing in New Zealand
By Kris Kjeldsen of Moana Nui

One person waka ama (W1) racing in New Zealand has been limited to flat water sprint racing until recently. In the past, there have been a few medium distance races (up to fifteen kilometre) on rivers or tidal estuaries and the canoes used were the same flat water designs as for sprint racing.

With the design and production of the *Surfrigger* solo canoe two years ago by Moana Nui, a canoe specific to the needs of rough ocean conditions or surf, interest in solo ocean racing is growing – as it is in Hawaii and Australia.

In Hawaii, most solo canoes are designed for rough, down wind conditions with surf and are fitted with rudders, whilst in Tahiti, the home of one person outrigger canoe paddling, no rudders are used or allowed in racing.

In 1995 four of New Zealand's top canoe paddlers decided they would like to go to Hawaii to compete in Walter Guild's Kaiwi Challenge – a two person team race for solo canoes over forty miles, crossing the infamous Kaiwi Channel (Molokai).

Aotearoa paddlers were Maui Kjeldsen (my son), Bo Herbert, Rikky Nuu and Paul Wilford. Maui was the current NZ solo champion and the others have either already held that position or have been consistently number two or three. Maui, Bo and Rikky were also part of the nine man New Zealand team that finished second in the Hamilton Island marathon and fifth in the Bankoh Molokai Hoe in 1993. Maui was also the World Junior solo champion winning gold in that event at Sacramento.

In 1992, they all owned *Surfriggers* and started training in all kinds of conditions to prepare for Hawaii. Because of the growing interest in this type of racing and as a lead up to the Kaiwi Challenge in May, I organised The Tutukaka Coast Ocean Canoe

Debbie Halkyard

Challenge in March – twenty-five kilometres of open ocean along the ruggedly beautiful Tutukaka coast near Whangarei in the north of the North Island.

This successful event will now become annual. Maui finished first in the outrigger division with Paul second and Bo third. Rikky competed in the surf ski division.

As a result of the event, Surfsports, an offshoot of Auckland Surf Lifesaving Association, included an outrigger division in a long distance surf ski race held in Auckland Harbour in April. Once again, Maui won, with Paul, Bo and Rikky finishing in that order.

Kaiwi Challenge – Hawaii

Those two races and other trials were used to select Maui and Paul to paddle together as team one and Bo and Rikky as team two for the Kaiwi Challenge. I got the job as manager and with some sponsorship help, we were off to Hawaii.

It was our intention to test the *Surfrigger* canoe in Hawaiian conditions, so with a lot of persuasion, Air New Zealand transported two, twenty-four foot canoes to Hawaii as part of our baggage!

One week before the Kaiwi Challenge event, we found ourselves being met at the airport by legendary canoe paddler, steerer and surfer, Nappy Napolean with his wife Anona – our hosts in Hawaii. The canoes were loaded on the roof, bags and bodies

loaded into the van and we were off to the start of a canoe race – the last in a series leading up to the Kaiwi Challenge.

This was an individual race, so Nappy had arranged for two Hawaiian style canoes to enable all four boys to race. There were divisions for surf skis or outrigger canoes as well as a choice of a long course (Kailua to Waikiki) or short course (Portlock to Waikiki). In their jet-lagged state, the boys opted for the shorter distance.

The weather on the day and the course, indicated relatively protected, calm water which is just what they got. Maui and Bo took the Hawaiian canoes and Rikky and Paul took the two *Surfriggers,* which go well in both flat and rough conditions.

The *Surfrigger* design is a compromise worked out for New Zealand racing requirements, that is, competitive in flat water sprints as well as the open ocean. The Hawaiian designs are all more specialised and come into their own in rough, down wind conditions and surf.

Maui ended up finishing first, with Paul and Rikky around fourth and fifth. Both of them had decided to catch a little lift on small waves breaking over a reef at the turn into Outrigger Canoe Club. They hadn't anticipated the water to be quite as shallow as it was and both ended up stopped dead with their rudders jammed into the coral! (There's nothing like a little local knowledge.) As manager, it was my job

Pre-start warm up, Kaiwi Channel

Paul Wilford

Bo Herbert

later on in the evening to repair the canoes and so ended our first day in paradise.

We spent the week acclimatizing, training off Waikiki, sightseeing and meeting people with Nappy, or surfing with him at Waikiki on boards and canoes. Evenings were spent at his home, listening to his many stories reflecting on a life-time of surfing, canoe paddling and sailing.

A day before the event, we flew over to Molokai to relax. Conditions all around the island had been pretty flat the whole week. Not much wind and not much swell. There were no waves at all at the west end of the island where the race was to start, but a swell was being predicted for the weekend.

On Saturday morning we awoke to drizzling rain and south-west winds with about one to two foot surf. At midday we walked down to the beach and there were some four to five footers building up. Maui decided to go for a body surf and had a run in with a big set and some coral reef.

By the afternoon, the rest of the

competitors and canoes were starting to arrive. Everyone spent the afternoon and evening watching the surf which had built to as much as ten foot. We wondered how they would get the canoes out through it the next morning.

Sunday morning and the surf had dropped back a little, but still around four to six feet. The wind had shifted back to north-east trades blowing to twenty-five knots. While the escort boats with relief paddlers were coming around from Hale O Lono harbour, the starting paddlers were waiting for lulls in the surf to get outside. This process took about one and a half hours for everyone to get outside the surf line, and ready for the start. The women were followed by the men.

Conditions made it pretty exciting. The main swell from the north was from the wrong direction to offer any lifts, but the trades on top of the swells made for some pretty good surfing.

Maui in team one, started and the first

Kaiwi Channel change-over, Maui and Paul

Ah! Tahiti. A place of pilgrimage for any devoted outrigger canoeist.
Maui Kjeldsen in a Tahitian va'a before the start of the Super Aito 1995

change occurred after half an hour. Paul was a bit disoriented at first and flipped the canoe once in his first stint, but after that he got more into the rhythm of the waves as the race progressed. Bo was the first paddler in team two and he and Maui were placed in the first five at the start.

Some paddlers went north, some went south, and some, like our teams, decided that straight across was the best course. Actually, our guys took a course curving slightly north of the rum line. As the pack spread out it was hard to tell where anyone stood in relation to the others.

Once the canoes started converging off Koko Head it became apparent that the northerly course was probably the best. Even though Maui and Paul were passing quite a few other canoes, they finished eighth overall in about five and a half hours. Bo and Rikky finished about twentieth from fifty three teams.

Super Aito − Tahiti

Near the end of August, Maui and I received a fax from Maara Pitpmai and Charley Maitere, the organisers of the Budweiser Channel Wa'a or Super Aito

race which crosses the channel from the island of Moorea to Point Venice on Tahiti. They had spoken to Maui about participating in the thirty kilometre race for solo canoes without rudders, when we were in Apia for the 1994 Worlds.

This is a race for the top twenty-five Tahitian men paddling single canoes. They first have to qualify in the Aito − a twenty kilometre race, partly in the lagoon and partly outside. From the two hundred or so competitors in the Aito, the first twenty-five qualify for the Super Aito or Bud Channel Va'a. Some paddlers are also invited from other countries.

Maara and Charley arranged for Air New Zealand to fly Maui, Aaron Herbert (Bo's younger brother and Junior World Champ) and myself at a discount rate. They also arranged for our stay at the Pirae Canoe Club as guests of Edward Mamaatua and lent us Charley's ute.

A few days before we were due to fly, all hell broke loose at Fa'aa Airport in Papeete. On Friday we got a phone call from Maara that they were trying to postpone the race to the next week when, hopefully, things would have settled down. On Saturday night we received another call to catch our flight the next day.

Arriving at Fa'aa we were surprised to see that there appeared not to be much damage either at the airport or in Papeete. We spent the week trying out different canoes and training. Tahiti seemed just as it always was, with no obvious trouble and business as usual. Unfortunately, Hawaiian Airlines cancelled the flight that would have brought the two Foti brothers who had also been invited to compete.

Maui and Aaron tried canoes, rigging and ama during the week and made their final choices. It was also necessary to have spray suits made. On Saturday morning we boarded one of the ferries to take us across the channel to Moorea with the canoes.

We were glad to see that the wind was from the south and quite fresh with some good size waves running in the right direction. It looked like there would be good surfing and a fast race,

The rules were one man, one va'a and one support boat. Escort boats had to stay behind until paddlers were out in the ocean, beyond the reef and spreading out. Contact between escort boat and paddler was to be only fifteen minutes on the hour for supply of water, food and spare paddles.

As soon as we could after the start the escort boat raced after Maui. The pack was spreading out and it looked like Maui was in a group out front; neck and neck with a couple of paddlers to the south and a few more northwards.

Different theories as to what was the best course abounded. Some paddlers took a southern course across to Pa'aa Point then followed the reef around past Papeete to Point Venus. Some took a more northerly and straight line course. Maui, after considering the options decided to go slightly south, but head directly for Papeete and then follow the reef to the finish.

On reaching the open ocean, conditions were quite rough with large seas, but the wind had dropped a little. During the race the continuing wind and swell were such that not much surfing was possible.

Unfortunately Aaron had to pull out with severe leg cramps caused partly by an ill-fitting spray suit which restricted his leg movements. He had also been training over the cold New Zealand winter in a solo canoe with rudder. The heat, the distance, the lack of rudder and the spray suit all took their toll. He felt that it was the hardest, most painful race he had ever done.

As paddlers started to converge near Papeete sea wall, it looked like Maui might still be in the top five. As the support boat neared, it became apparent that he was in

Start of the Super Aito 1995

TAHITI HOE HANDCRAFTS LARGE OUTRIGGER CANOE
"STEERING PADDLES" FROM THE EXOTIC WOODS OF THE SOUTH SEAS.

Nostalgic

Over 35 different templates are used to reproduce true, historic Hawaiian and Tahitian style steering paddles. When laminating various species of 20 different woods to the above templates, we virtually guarantee that no two paddles will be exactly alike.
These replicas are reproduced from authentic, original paddles and are truly "Big" and "Beautiful" reminders of old Oceania.

Decorative

Although epoxy laminations insure full functional use, these paddles are designed for use as "wallhangers" in the office, dens, clubhouses and restaurants for the outrigger canoe crowd.

WE AIRSHIP TO ANYWHERE IN THE WORLD.
FOR A BROCHURE AND MORE INFORMATION, WRITE OR FAX TO:

TAHITI

PO Box 14185, 98701, Arue
Tahiti, French Polynesia
Tel 689 482 707
Fax 689 483 091

HAWAII

PO Box 3054, Honolulu
Hawaii, 96802 USA
Tel 808 737 1117
Fax 808 737 2752

Maui Kjeldsen Moorea, Tahiti.

The sea running blue and all around, silence.

fact fifth – and his tiredness became obvious – but so it was with the paddlers in front. With encouragement Maui found some reserves of energy and started the hard work of picking up a place or two.

After a few hundred metres and a couple of good wave lifts he caught and passed Karyl Moani About a mile later, Maui caught Robo Bernproino and put himself in third position to the finish.

The first finisher was Conrad van Bastolaer who did the event in 2:47:50. Second was Franco Taraihau in 2:52:38. Maui, third, in 2:54:02. Lewis Lauglin, winner of the three previous Super Aito events was not racing this year because in the qualifying Aito race he put his canoe on

a reef and did not finish. Lewis' best time for the race was 2:50:33 in 1993.

First prize was US$4,000 and Maui won US$500 for third. This race is definitely a challenge.

Oceans Sea Kayak Challenge – Aotearoa

A couple of weeks after the Super Aito, the second annual Oceans Sea Kayak Classic was held at Matauri Bay in the north of the North Island. This year, as well as the sea kayak division, there were divisions for single outrigger and surf ski.

The course was in and around the picturesque and rugged Cavalli Islands and back to Matauri Bay – a distance of about thirty kilometres for the men. The course

Presentations Super Aito 1995 – Budweiser Channel Va'a. Who's the white guy?

New Zealand. a place of outstanding scenic beauty and ruggedness.

Paul Wilford, first finisher in the Oceans Sea Kayak Classic rounding Hole in the Rock, Cavalii Islands (above) and (below) Matauri Bay.

zig-zagged around the islands. Some legs were up wind and swell, some down wind and some side-on to both sea and wind. On the day the wind was about fifteen to twenty knots with a bumpy swell especially on the outer side of the islands as a result of twenty to thirty knots the day before.

In the Men's outrigger division, Paul Wilford took first. Maui took a close second to Shaun Reese (South Africa) in the men's surf ski division. Corrina Gage finished first with Anna Croonshaw second in the women's outrigger event – both were part of the New Zealand Women's team that went to Tahiti last April.

The solo outrigger long distance racing year wound up with a thirty kilometre race on the Waikato River from Hamilton to Huntly. Corrina Gage once again taking out the Women's division. The Men's was won by my son-in-law, Stuart Wilson with Turi Hodges finishing second.

ON THE SAME DAY RIKI MATENGA OF GISBORNE AND CONRAD EDWARDS OF WELLINGTON CROSSED THE COOK STRAIT IN *SURFRIGGER* CANOES ENCOUNTERING THIRTY KNOT WINDS FOR PART OF THE WAY AND CONFUSED SEAS CAUSED BY TIDAL CURRENTS WHICH RUN BETWEEN THE 'TWO ISLANDS. THIS IS THE FIRST SUCH CROSSING IN SOLO WAKA AMA IN MODERN TIMES.

It's been a good first year of open ocean, long distance, solo waka ama racing which looks set to be a major part of outrigger canoeing in Aotearoa.

Whitsunday Fibreglass

The Original Home of The Classic Canoe in Australia

Whitsunday Fibreglass pride themselves on being instrumental in the growth and development of outrigger canoe racing in Australia through the manufacture of eighty percent of six-person outrigger canoes in Australia since 1989.

We also take pride in manufacturing our canoes to the highest possible standards. Canoes are completely hand-laid and in addition are manufactured with navigational light brackets and built in safety compartments for stowage of safety equipment.

We offer two canoe types - The Classic and The Corbishley which includes a wider seat at number one, improved wae (spreaders) for iako attachment and a seamless deck.

All canoes are guaranteed to be within two kilograms of one hundred and fifty kilograms and are surveyed and approved by the Department of Transport

We provide a full repair and refurbishment service including two pac canoe and ama resprays and iako re-sand and coating.

Whitsunday Fibreglass
Hawaiian Class Racer experts in Australia
committed to manufacturing quality outrigger canoeing products.

Photo Barry Alsop

Out on a Limb...

Ama Design in Transition Walter Guild on Ama

You manufacture the Channel Master ama. What prompted you to design a different shape?

Actually Tom Connor built an ama that we used and won in the 1986 Moloka'i Channel race. It was a departure from the traditional banana shaped ama as it had a flatter bottom. It was definitely an early prototype though, being considerably different to what we have now in the Channel Master.

Some of the design remained similar. A longer water line, flatter bottom, higher front neck, a pedestal at the back to get the rear iako up away from the water, holes through that for lashing and the front was still lashed right around. It was the beginning of a realisation that there was something faster than the banana ama.

We learned some things with that ama using it in the Moloka'i in 1986 and 1987 and winning both years using it. Hank Lass, our partner here at the Fiberglass Shop at the time, contracted Joe Quigg to build a prototype of his idea of a new ama and Joe came up with the Channel Master.

> *"You can have a great primary hull with a lousy ama and you're not going to reach your full potential"*

Tom Connor's Moby Dick ama, with similar neck and lupe as above, was one of the first attempts to improve upon the traditional banana style.

The Moby ama was quite massive (hence the name). It was considerably straighter through the mid-section so that it floated rather than sank, and had a longer water line length.

The inclusion of lashing holes prevented the lashing from making contact with the undersurface of the ama thereby eliminating additional drag. A pedestal was included upon which the iako sat.

Outrigger Canoe Club Hawaii won the Moloka'i in '86 and '87 using the Moby Dick ama, proving its validity as a design improvement over the banana style ama.

Joe Quigg was then contracted to design a new ama based on what had been learnt and also on the feedback from crews. So the Channel Master was created.

Now it is supplied standard on all Hawaiian Class Racer and Force 5 canoes and has been an extremely popular design. Below, a Channel Master ama awaiting finishing touches.

Hank at the time was paddling Senior Masters at the Outrigger. They paddled with it then gave it to me to try. I realised it was exceptional, being way better than the production ama of the time.

So we went ahead and Brent Bixler built the mould incorporating all hole-tied lashing points front and rear so as all the cordage would be free of the water. That has done really, really well – paddlers seem to like it as an all around ama. Today it is the standard ama supplied with both the "Classic" and Force 5 canoes.

We seem to be seeing an increasing number of ama designs around – one-offs and production models. Can it be said that the reality is we need a different ama for different conditions? For example it has been my experience that for sprint or regatta races the banana style ama is excellent in turns while the longer flatter style tends to go straight. Do we need a quiver of ama for a variety of conditions?

Yeah, that would be ideal. We will see increasingly more ama designs being tried. It is very difficult to design an ama and a hull both in the development stage at the same time.

The ama is a very important factor, more so than many have thought. We at this shop look at them as separate hulls. Your potential is limited by either one. You can have a great primary hull and a lousy ama and you're not going to reach your full potential.

Therefore what we would do is develop a constant at one end – for instance the ama – and to test hull design, have the same ama used on two different hulls. Once we establish that this is the best we can do with

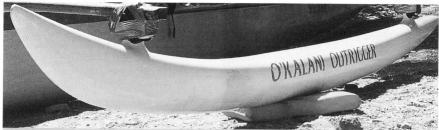

Check these out - variations on a theme. These are two ama photographed in California on Catalina Island and are for very different paddling environments. The above has plenty of forward rocker to prevent nose diving with a vee'd bow to splice cleanly through oncoming waves and a reasonably long straight water line section not dissimilar to the Channel Master.

The ama below is without doubt a flat water device with rounded front section and almost a flat top deck, resembling a stretched dinghy profile. The raised iako pedestal would, if hit by an oncoming wave, absorb a terrific amount of shock with the wide surface area exposed. What is interesting about this lashing method is that the iako is lashed parallel to the lashing holes. Once you understand how certain design criteria affect performance in particular conditions, you can begin to draw your own conclusions about how any one ama design may perform just by taking a close look at it.

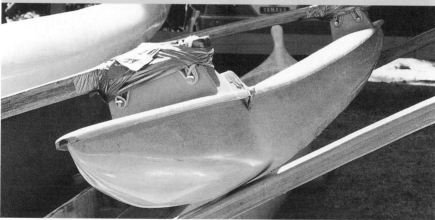

the hull, then we go back and keep the hull constant while we change the ama. This is what we did in relation to the design of the Kaiwi Challenger solo canoe and found that to be very successful as we upgraded things. It is very difficult to be in a state of flux with both at the same time.

It seems ama are definitely not given enough credit for the degree to which they affect overall

performance and handling?

We really learned this with the solo canoes. It didn't become that evident until we started our testing with ama for the Kaiwi Challenger. We were amazed at how much faster we could go with the ama in the air.

That told us that the way in which the ama makes contact with the water and the way in which it's rigged and sits on the water is critical to hull speed.

49

The Californian designed Pacific Islander ama, is an architectural masterpiece. Its forward lupe section is something to behold and all with good reason. Its primary function being to raise the forward iako well clear of the water so oncoming waves avoid crashing into it. Its waterline length however is not unlike the traditional banana styled ama with a curvature continuing well clear of the exit point at the rear. As it is designed, the forward neck section would absorb a lot of shock.

The Catamaran ama developed by the Offshore California Club is exactly that - a design modelled on a Hobie Cat pontoon. Based on the logical theory that catamarans are fast, stable craft and that their pontoons have been carefully refined over years of research and development to be hydrodynamically efficient so why not adapt it into an outrigger ama.

It does work well but not in rough water – specifically big water. It's hard lines and knife like design make it very good at tracking (holding a straight line), however, if it takes a swell on the beam it wants to trip over itself by digging in deep and biting, causing excessive strain on the iako to ama lashing and back to the canoe spreaders. This in turn stalls the canoe's progress (where a rounded profile ama will slide out minimizing strain).

The Catamaran ama is fundamentally an exercise in minimilization, good for some conditions but not all. Its overall superstructure is streamlined and low with slight rocker fore and aft and a hard, chined vee undersection for the first quarter. These clean lines make a fast, staight line ama which doesn't react well to adverse sideways torque caused by wave action on the canoe's beam.

Ama design is in transition. Here's the reality. You need a quiver of ama for a whole variety of conditions. Ama for regatta/sprint races in flat water, long swell, short swell, wind chop, downwind and upwind – and all-round ama is ultimately a compromise and never specific to any given condition.

A quiver of ama is clearly cheaper than a quiver of canoes – providing a cost effective means of improving the handling qualities of your canoe. The ama is the *other* hull with a specific purpose which needs to be in every way as efficient as the canoe hull itself. Whilst its primary purpose is to act as a counterpoise, you should not lose sight of the fact that it represents drag and needs therefore to be as hydrodynamically efficient as possible. Below; Channel Master.

BLADERUNNER BOATS SYDNEY 02 544 1401

Manufacturers of Outrigger Canoes, Racing and Surfing Accessories

The Bladerunner OC6 built to AOCRA specifications is a new addition to the Australian race circuit and has already enjoyed several race victories in the Sydney region.

At 45' the Bladerunner is longer than the Classic canoe. With extended rocker fore and aft the Bladerunner picks up runners easily and is generally very responsive.

Excellent lateral and longitudinal strength, make for a stiff hull. Additionally, a strong keel area prevents point of load damage common to conventional layups, with stronger gunwales, iako mounts, water tight compartments providing positive floatation. Colour combinations to suit your requirements.

"Quality is an Advantage"

BLADERUNNER BOATS: C/-JOHN HAYES

13 DAROOK PARK RD CRONULLA AUSTRALIA NSW 2230 PH/FAX: 02 544 1401

Todd Bradley on the Zen of Steering

Todd Bradley spent much of his youth growing up around Honolulu and the Outrigger Canoe Club of Hawaii; the club for whom he steers today.

Paddling since a young kid, Todd Bradley realized by his early teens that his future was in steering. Since then, he has dedicated himself to mastering the art. The steerer has arguably, the most demanding of positions in an outrigger canoe.

Bearing in mind the Outrigger Canoe Club's status in the world of outrigger canoeing, its history of association with the sport, and the degree to which the club's reputation and esteem rests on the performance of its teams, you can be assured that Todd's position as steerer for the senior men, makes him one of the best.

Today, Todd should be acknowledged as one of the finest exponents of the skill. His style and approach to steering epitomizing what would seem to be essential attributes in a master at the task.

HIS ABILITY TO STAY FULLY FOCUSED AS HE WORKS THE CANOE AMONGST SWELLS, WHILST MOTIVATING AND DIRECTING HIS CREW, IS ONE THAT CAN ONLY BE DESCRIBED AS SPOOKY. TRANSFIXED AND POSSESSED BY THE OCEAN ENVIRONMENT, HE CONTINUALLY ADJUSTS THE CANOE TO ANY NUANCES OF THE OCEAN – WORKING ITS ENERGY FOR ALL IT'S WORTH.

The dying moments of the 1994 Bankoh Moloka'i race truly lifted Todd's status to one of the sport's great exponents of the art. Outrigger was locked in a dual for second and third spot with Dana Point, California as they entered Waikiki Bay. After nearly

Todd Bradley – Hamilton Cup, Australia 1995. Intense from start to finish . . .

five hours of steering, Todd's strength of character, judgement and experience shone through as he took the canoe on an inside course and allowed Dana to pull away. The crowd on the beach thought he had lost the plot, when from the ocean depths a swell arose and lifted the canoe and thundered it past Dana who must have been broken men at this point.

Fred Hemmings, one of Hawaii's canoeing legends who paddled with the late Duke Kahanamoku, commented to a long time friend of Todd's, Greg Moss, that Todd had undoubtedly made the transition from good steerer to outstanding.

The steerer's lot is not a happy one for much of the time. It seems that when things go well, the steerer is hailed a hero or at least allowed to share in the same adulation as fellow paddlers. If on the other hand things don't go so well, the steerer is best to leave the beach as quickly and

discreetly as possible before the post-mortem on where things went wrong begins to get ugly.

Unless you really understand the complexities of what it takes to be a steerer, even of average standing, you should perhaps look elsewhere for the blame. After all the steerer is in a position from which all can be seen and is not without an opinion as to how things went.

This being said, the steerer needs to have skin like a rhino in order to deflect the shots being fired; to avoid being mortally wounded and thereby giving up in the steep part of the learning curve at the beginning of a steering career. Many would-be steerers don't continue long for this very reason; deciding to take the safe option of paddling.

A steerer must be assertive with decisions in regard to how best to steer a course and equally assertive in giving crew

Tom Connor steering for Hawaii Team Masters at the 1995 Hamilton Cup International Race, Australia. Note the double bent-shaft paddle and the relaxed look despite losing their support boat, driving rain and choppy seas! Tom took up outrigging in 1968 but did not take up steering until 1980. Now, sixteen years and eleven Moloka'i victories later . . .

direction and support. The steerer is the only one who gets to rubber-neck during the race and the only one who can truly assess how the canoe is travelling and how the crew is performing.

A steerer must gain the respect of paddlers so that the crew will listen to the game plan and respond when asked for more power or different stroke rates or given words of encouragement. To this end a crew should put themselves in the hands of the steerer because generally speaking the canoe is at the steerer's mercy.

I suppose that in this respect you might feel completely justified in blaming a steerer for a poor result, after all, they are at the controls, calling the shots. The steerer however is not the engine room, that's the job of the other five. Whilst the steerer aims to get the most out of paddlers, out of the canoe and its interaction with the ocean, they cannot be held accountable for everything. It's hard to soar like an eagle when you work with turkeys.

TO WATCH AN EXPERT STEERING AN OUTRIGGER CANOE IN A HEAVING OCEAN IS TO WATCH SOMEONE WHO HAS DEVELOPED A CLOSENESS WITH AND UNDERSTANDING OF THE OCEAN ENVIRONMENT, AS WELL AS KNOWLEDGE OF THE WAY IN WHICH THE CANOE WILL RESPOND TO EACH WAVE. AT THIS LEVEL, STEERING BECOMES AN ART FORM. WORKING WITH THE POWER OF THE OCEAN AND NOT AGAINST IT.

When a steerer positions the canoe on a runner in order to surf down the face (no matter how small) they will have achieved speed which no amount of paddle power could hope to do. The ocean's power far exceeds that of human beings; an understanding which the Polynesians had thousands of years ago.

TO HARNESS NATURE'S ENERGY AND USE IT TO ADVANTAGE IN A CANOE CONSIDERED THE GREATEST ROUGH-WATER OCEAN CRAFT EVER DEVISED, REQUIRES A SENSE OF TOUCH AND DELICACY WHICH IS CLEARLY ON A HIGHER LEVEL OF THOUGHT THAN BRUTE STRENGTH.

Watching Tom Connor and Todd Bradley steering in rough, chaotic water at Australia's Hamilton Cup event, and Jim Foti steering in the '95 Moloka'i, my perspective on steering changed radically. A revelation was at hand watching from the complete discomfort of heaving support boats. I felt I was in the presence of brilliance. And I was. (Which incidentally helped ease my seasickness.)

Though all different in their styles Tom, Todd and Jim looked completely at ease and in total control of their canoes at all times. No matter what the ocean had to throw at them. Paddle and blade strokes were executed with deliberate placement and delicacy, designed to set the canoe up to make the most of every bump and depression.

The ocean through their eyes is clearly very different to what it is to many others. Not just a rough and distorted waterscape to be carved through, but a vast watery carpet full of valuable kinetic energy, used to advantage in making the canoe go from a relative state of momentum into bursts of acceleration, whereby the paddlers get relief and the canoe surges ahead on a free ride.

I find it hard to contain my enthusiasm for excellence and revelation when it is encountered.

Todd Bradley has kindly taken time to share some insights into the finer points of better steering. . .

An Interview with Todd Bradley

Todd Bradley doing what he does best. Steering at the 1995 'Skippy' race from Hawaii Kai to Barbers Point. Funny as it may seem, with such a massive crew in front of him, Todd has to lean way out to see around backs like barn doors, in order to check they're on line, all the time being careful not to affect stability. Just one of the many difficulties (some steerers at least) have to overcome!

When did you begin paddling?

I started when I was twelve, paddling and steering whenever they needed help. So over time I picked it up. I paddled Moloka'i for the first time when I was eighteen and have paddled it over fifteen times, including five times on the solo. And every Kona race since I was eighteen.

When did you make the decision to steer full time?

I was stroke for the Eighteen boys yet in the Sixteen's I steered, so it really happened as I advanced into the upper division men and I guess it happened because of my size. Having always been with the Outrigger Club, I grew up around guys like Tommy Connor and Brant Ackerman. I was the second crew steersman for eight years and the same number of Moloka'i crossings, whilst Tommy steered the first crew.

How was it knowing that Tom Connor was the guy you had to aspire to replace?

It was tough. he is definitely something of a legend here in Hawaii. Tommy has steered possibly more Outrigger Canoe Club victories than any one in its history – not to mention all of his Moloka'i victories. For many years I steered the first crew for the first part of the season during regattas (sprints), then with the start of the distance season Tommy would take over.

To what degree did Tom Connor help and influence you?

It was mostly through watching and trying always to be better. I didn't actually get much coaching. It was more through criticism and the mental confidence to learn, improve and get better; always trying different things and listening to what

Solo paddling has helped me immensely – probably more than anything – to improve my steering.

One thing a steerer enjoys is having plenty of power in the canoe when they need it, especially in catching the runners. Todd certainly enjoys steering with paddlers he knows will give a total commitment. In addition to this, steering for those who also paddle solo makes all the difference as they are intuitively aware of when the canoe is onto a swell and they work it for all it's worth without necessarily having to be prompted. They know better than anyone, the rewards of a free ride!

The steerer's role as captain is paramount. Too many decision-makers is definitely a recipe for disaster. Underlying the role of steerer as leader, there needs to be an undercurrent in the canoe akin to a mutual admiration society. Mutual respect is essential. Know your role in the canoe, perform it to the best of your ability and everyone stays happy . . . most of the time!

people had to say. Walter Guild has been a great help being extremely knowledgeable. Solo paddling has helped me immensely to improve, probably more than anything else.

Is this because of the intimacy with the ocean that you get paddling solo?

Yeah, learning to surf the bumps by yourself.

Does this explain why many steerers tend to make good solo paddlers?

Absolutely. Both the Foti brothers of Lanikai OCC are steerers and two of the best Hawaiian solo paddlers, Walter Guild and Marc Hain are both excellent solo paddlers. Steerers have a feel for the canoe. This I believe is something that can't be taught. You either have it or you don't. You need time in the boat and an understanding of what's going on around and under you whilst on the water . . . and the ability to make something out of it.

So what would you describe as being the qualities a steerer should have in order to excel?

Well anyone can be taught to steer. But to learn to feel, anticipate and be at one with the ocean, to constantly find the sweet spot,

One thing that comes with experience is the steerer's ability to take risks and get away with it. Todd has certainly mastered this skill and reads the water brilliantly. Whilst many steerers shy away from rugged cliffs and submerged coral heads (and rightly so if inexperienced) Todd has tasted the rewards of sneaking around tight corners where others fear to venture. On one occasion I watched him turn the canoe and surf almost directly at the rock face surfing down a surging wave, turning away at the last moment and squeezing out the back door before the wave rushed back out to meet the next incoming. He gained fifty yards on the leading canoe.

take it and maximise it with the help of the five others in the canoe . . . that is another dimension. The sweet spot is always there. You just have to find it and it might not necessarily be directly downwind. You have to also be aware of the canoe's sweet spot and in this respect there are no hard and fast rules.

In essence, to go beyond just holding the canoe on course, you have to make the process an intellectual one and be in tune with ocean, canoe and crew?

Yeah. And at the end of a race, I feel more mentally drained than physically, having had to be fully focused holding the canoe

> ... it's how you react to the obstacles thrown in front of you. and the speed at which you react, that makes for a good steerer.
>
> TOM CONNOR

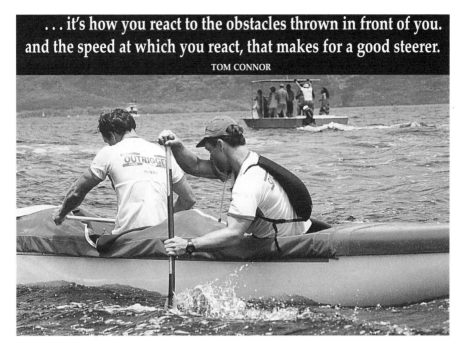

on course and finding the best course, whilst keeping an eye on the competition. As Tommy Connor once said to me, "it's how you react to the obstacles thrown in front of you and the speed at which you react, that makes for a good steerer." One thing I've learned to trust is my first instinctual judgement – which takes confidence, experience and ultimately, wisdom. This is an important transition for any steerer who has learned the skill well and is ready to become a great steerer.

Does the steerer make or break a race?

The steerer makes all the difference in the world. You can have great paddlers, but if the steerer doesn't put them in the right spot, they're stuffed. Then again, the steerer can be doing everything right but he needs to have a crew that are the best if the canoe is to cross the line first.

To what degree do you motivate and coach your crew?

All the time. They're always listening out for me to tell them what I'm feeling. Our crew is very much aware of how things are at any given moment. If I haven't spoken up for a while, they begin to wonder what's going on with me.

But for them to listen to you they need to respect you ...

That's the whole deal. And you only gain that respect over time – winning races and making judgment calls that work. You have to learn to be a leader who's trusted. Which can be tough. Sometimes however I feel I'm talking too much, particularly if all I have to say is negative about someone's technique or rhythm. Then it's best to go quiet for a while. Elite crews shouldn't have this problem anyhow; they are so in tune with their paddling that they rarely

Keeping the ama steady is crucial whenever poking on the offside as its response to the drag created is to lift. Here Todd buries the blade and eyeballs the ama whilst keeping his body weight and arm over to the ama side. Paddlers can only do their job well if the canoe feels stable. If it feels tippy then a level of stress and anxiety is present which does not make for relaxed, efficient paddling. In this respect the steerer has a great degree of affect on the canoe's stability and a responsibility to make sure the canoe remains as stable as possible.

need to be reminded and when they are told, they correct almost immediately.

Do you have a system of passing messages along the canoe or do you just yell?

Just yelling . . . unless it's noisy, then we have to pass the message along!

When I have watched you steer, there seems a delicacy of paddle placement and not much apparent steering going on?

Finesse is important. I'm not a motor I'm a rudder. But I have to be an efficient rudder so that every time I stick my paddle in the water, the drag I create steers the canoe. When I poke on the left side I create drag so the right side of the canoe will run. But you don't want to overdo the drag as the canoe will slow. All my moves have to be very subtle and I'm always anticipating how the canoe will react. If you let the canoe drop off course too much, it requires a lot of effort to correct it. Once forty-two feet of waterline decides where it wants to go, you're going to have to cause a lot of drag to stop it. So best to stop it before it goes . . . rather like balancing a ball on the end of your nose! You move left and right in anticipation of it falling off, to counteract the canoe's movement. With the introduction of the new Force 5 canoes their increased rocker, makes them easier to

Todd leaves a quiver of steering sticks on the support boat, frequently changing paddles as the conditions alter. Here he is throwing away what you might think are perfectly workable paddles and retrieving another passed up to him by a swimmer in the water. These choices come with experience and in knowing which blade will best suit any given conditions – giving you an idea to what level you might aspire. The bottom line here is that Todd is a perfectionist, who wants to be the best he can and to achieve this, it's essential that his paddles perform at an optimum level.

steer and easier to turn. But they are very responsive so that oversteer is a real problem when you make the transition from the Hawaiian Class Racer (Classic).

I've heard people say that when the canoe falls off course, you're better to leave it – see if it corrects itself?

That's what I do. Why fight it, you're only going to cause more drag and use more energy up if it's fallen off course only a little. Let it run and find its own way back and sometimes this is a good way to find the sweet spot on the canoe, given the conditions and the crew weight. The fastest line between two points is not always straight. Falling off and rounding up continually along a leg can pay off with the extra speed you get. Nothing's faster than a runaway canoe. A runaway canoe is cooking even at an angle. Control it and use it to your advantage!

How much of the time, as a steerer, do you spend paddling?

When I do paddle, I need to paddle with finesse. If you're a strong paddler at six and you start going for it, the five others who are trying to find and maintain rhythm, may think this feels good all of a sudden. Then you have to poke and they feel the change and begin to wonder what's going on. Better to keep it smooth and not kick in too

Nothing's faster than a runaway canoe. A runaway canoe is cooking even at an angle. Control it and use it to your advantage!

hard. Help them out a little but don't upset their rhythm. You are not there to be part of the motor.

Many would say that the steerer should be a sixth paddler as much as possible?

Perhaps in the flat water and in regatta (sprint) racing but not in open ocean racing where you should be focusing on looking for runners. The ocean's energy is far greater than any stroke you can take. You really make little difference by paddling.

To what degree does a steerer dictate the capsize of a canoe?

A lot. You have to consider that the drag a steerer creates on the right side causes the left side to lift up, taking the ama with it. When I'm poking on the right side, I twist and extend my arm over the left. I can't remember ever tipping in a race, so I guess I have it wired. When I do paddle, I paddle eighty-five percent of the time on the left to keep the ama down. If I'm poking on the right side and the ama lifts, I quickly

A paddle quiver – a paddle for all occasions and all conditions. Todd designs and constructs all of his own paddles. Its cheaper this way in the long run, if you really want to experiment and get exactly what you're looking for. All you need are the right tools and the willingness to learn and make a few stuff ups along the way. Todd makes his paddles under his Hawaiian name of Pohaku (strong, like rock) and he makes them exactly like that. He's not in the habit of manufacturing on any large scale, making only about twenty a year for others, including his own crew and for friends.

Whilst he admits they look a little on the rugged side, they are functional and you can guarantee, strong, using in combination with selected timbers, carbon graphite, which he adds to various structural stress points on the paddle relative to its function.

In many of his steering paddles, he splits the shaft the full length and sandwiches a layer of carbon between the two halves and when bonded together he'll add a wrap of carbon around the lower shaft to protect it and add additional strength. Net result, a bloody stiff shaft!

Mostly surfers make the best steerers. Catching waves is what they live for. They understand the dynamics of it all.

change and poke on the left to shut the ama down. Paddling on the right definitely makes the canoe unstable, which makes one through five back off the power. The more stable the canoe, the more relaxed the crew can be to paddle efficiently.

What injuries are common?

Hip problems seem to be common, because of the contortions. Also shoulders, neck and lower back which seems to relate to an over-developed left side twisting the body. The left side of my upper body is up to half an inch larger than the right. Solo paddling and gym workouts help to balance this. And plenty of massage!

Which sports compliment a steerer's training?

Mostly surfers make the best steerers. Catching waves is what they live for. They understand the dynamics of it all. They understand how a wave forms and can therefore anticipate its birth. Once the wave is there ahead of you it's too late.

How do you recognise the formation of a runner ahead of you?

Aiming for the low spots is crucial. Don't look over your shoulder. It's all ahead of you and within about a fifteen degree radius either side. Theoretically, the swells are travelling slower than you are. Waves are going up and down rather than forward. You have to look for the bump that is just being born. That's the one that will give you the money – it's anticipation. I have to coincide with the wave's initial formation so that as we pass over, it will kick in from behind and lift us. Then I tell the guys we're on it and they do the rest.

Is it harder to catch big waves?

Harder by far. Small swells and chop give you constant assistance: you can always find the sweet spot. Whilst big swells don't give you that consistency.

You make your own paddles . . .

I think its important if you want to find the right blade given any ocean condition and the variety of canoes you find yourself in, be it a Hawaiian Class Racer (Classic), Bradley or Force 5. The paddle is your only link with the ocean; your sole means of

At far left is a length of 3x2 which will eventually become the shaft. In the middle is a shaft template which has the last section from the neck to its tip planed into a wedge, of an angle which corresponds to the blade angle required. Todd prefers only a slight angle of 5-7 degrees. This template then forms the basis for all bent shaft paddles of its degree.

control. So how can I make my job easier? The more efficient the blade, the less effort needed to execute an effective stroke. Making my paddles gives me the chance to make my own designs at less expense whilst creating a tool that I can rely on to do what I want it to do.

So what will dictate the design of your paddle?

In flat water I'll use a small blade area and paddle a lot, whilst in rough water I'll use a progressively larger blade and paddle less. Shaft angle is the same as the crew (we don't use anything over seven degrees) so when I do paddle, my paddle is having the same effectiveness as the others. Different shaft angles means different power applications happening at different areas along the canoe length. Only my blade template differs. I always use a short shaft because of ease of use and the frequency at which I change sides. Less shaft equals less weight – and it's more manageable.

Your paddles are extremely stiff. How do you achieve this and why?

Stiff paddle shafts are essential. Whether you're paddling or steering, you want the canoe to react immediately and not have a delay period as the shaft bends and kicks in. I split my shafts and then sandwich them together with carbon graphite. Then sometimes I'll add a wrap around the outer lower and mid shaft region to protect it from abrasion and increase its stiffness. This eliminates delayed reactions when it's in the water and gives a positive feel.

Thanks for sharing your knowledge and experience with us.

Todd's workshop at home. The two paddles at left are taken from the late Duke Kahanamoku's steering paddle that is kept at the Outrigger Canoe Club of Hawaii. Made in Koa these were both destined for ornamental use.

Once the shaft has been routed into an oval or rounded section and the wedged blade portion planned, the different sections of hard and softwood timbers are cut into strips and glued firmly together to form a strong lamination.

Perfect glue lines are crucial so as no weak spots are created allowing the timbers to be bonded or laminated firmly against each other.

Once this is done, the blade shape template is laid over the blade area and marked out, then cut using a hand held band saw as seen here.

Todd selects Basswood, Ash or Koa for his shafts for strength and stiffness, which he will often split and sandwich a layer of carbon-fibre in between for additional strength – just to be sure! The blade itself will often be of Koa and Pine or Basswood reinforced in parts with carbon-fibre particularly around the tip.

After the template shape for the blade is cut the shaping is finished off with a belt sander and the edges also shaped. Skill and care is needed at this point so as not to take too much off. Once this is complete Todd prefers to coat the paddle only with an epoxy which he has perfected to produce a fantastic gloss finish.

Todd has made paddles from Hau (Sea Hibiscus) which he cuts into strips and laminates back together again, producing a strong lightweight paddle. He has also made iako for a single person outrigger in this way.

From the left a sexy looking placement of carbon strips and a carbon inlay along the length of the shaft, followed by a teardrop blade with carbon reinforcement over the tip and wrapped around the lower shaft. Next to this a much larger blade for canoe surfing and sailing with a vee of carbon across the face and a heavy shaft that keeps much of its thickness to the tip of the blade rather than being fared down progressively from the top of the blade. Beside this a solid blade with no laminations. Different constructions for different functions.

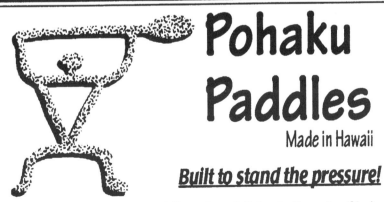

Concept II Indoor Rower

Early morning workout in the comfort of your own home. The Concept II Indoor Rower with "Sit and Switch" paddling adaptation, at last provides canoe sport enthusiasts with the dream machine for land-based paddling workouts. Just don't drip on the carpet!

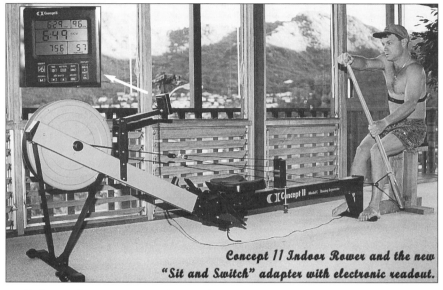

Concept II Indoor Rower and the new "Sit and Switch" adapter with electronic readout.

Each year there are many products and innovations which find their way into the market place – some good, some bad.

One product which has been in demand for quite some years is an adaptation for the universally well known "Rowing Machine" to suit single blade canoe sport enthusiasts. Whilst a kayak-style adaptation has been available, single-blade canoeists have had no such commercially available simulator to use.

Well at long last it has arrived through the creative talents of Mark McAndrew working alongside the manufacturers of the Concept II Indoor Rower, the world's foremost rowing style fitness machine often simply referred to as the "erg".

Although the original basis for modification was to accommodate white water slalom paddling, it never quite made that and instead it metamorphosed into a brilliant "Sit and Switch" land based fitness, endurance, strength and technique device, suitable for a wide range of single blade paddle-sport disciplines.

Whilst in Hawaii, it was my good fortune to stay with Todd Bradley, steerer for Outrigger Canoe Club who has a Concept II in his home where he was road testing the adaptation. The Outrigger Canoe Club also have one set up in their gym. Ever curious I just had to have a go – it is brilliant! I want one, and I want it now – was my reaction to this near-perfect piece of equipment.

It allows you to accurately simulate the same biomechanical motion used in paddling an outrigger canoe and the switch part presents no problems at all.

Additionally, via the Concept II Indoor Rower's electronic read out, you can set a paddling distance which counts down, telling you the distance pulled in each stroke. You can also set up interval training sets, at the end of which you can instantly have a reading of the results of each set and the averages. Whilst linked to a Polar heart monitor your heart rate can also be displayed.

All in all an outstanding package. If you don't

Here's another way to paddle indoors! Outrigger Canoe Club's tank allows two paddlers to work in sync. More a tool for coaches to analyse technique and working partnerships, than a strength, fitness, and endurance device.

have time to get down to the water to train, now you can literally paddle in your living room and achieve the same net effect.

Apart from the obvious benefits of using it for fitness, strength, endurance and technique training whether individually or under observation from a coach, the Outrigger Canoe Club of Hawaii has already used it to replace the "Time Trial" as one of the means of crew selection. This involves having a trialist paddle the canoe with a steerer over a set distance whilst being timed.

There are limitations with this methodology, the primary factor being the unpredictability of mother nature; wind gusts and tidal action never being constant. The simulator is used in a static environment in which conditions remain exactly the same for all trialists.

Mark McAndrew outlines the development of the Concept II Indoor Rower and talks about the implications for outrigger canoe land-based training as well as its suitability for other canoe sports.

Although I have never crossed the Kaiwi Channel or for that matter, even been in an outrigger canoe, much of my free time for the past twenty years has been spent paddling canoes. Marathon canoe racing has given me many enjoyable hours and played a major role in forming some life long friendships.

Most of my paddling and racing has been in the northeastern United States. Here rivers and lakes freeze over for the winter months making year-round on water training impossible. The idea of developing an off water training tool that could improve sport specific muscular strength, cardiovascular endurance and stroke technique became more attractive with every winter season.

Concept II has done a remarkable job since 1981 in designing and developing a machine that responded to these exact needs, but specifically for rowers not paddlers. The Concept II rowing machine turned out to be highly efficient and became a global standard.

While working at Concept II for the past five years I have learned much about the rowing machine and the benefits of training with it. I also received several requests from other paddlers familiar with the Concept II

Indoor Rower who were frustrated by the lack of any paddling machine. Realising the benefit paddlers could receive from rowing, I began work on an adaptation to the Concept II Indoor Rower that would allow someone owning one to both row and paddle it.

In the past year and a half prototypes of various stages of the adapter have been tested by outrigger, down river, marathon flat water and dragon boat racers and have performed exceptionally well for those disciplines. One such prototype is currently being used for a study being done on elite Hawaiian outrigger paddlers by Ron Hetzler PhD, an exercise physiologist at the University of Hawaii. Because the machines are calibrated identically, performances of different paddlers can be directly compared.

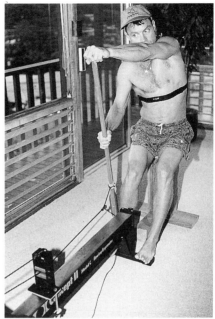

The adapter, designed for the Concept II model C Indoor Rower uses the same electronic monitor that is on the rower, allowing the paddler to keep track of strokes per minute, running time, distance rowed in meters, as well as the power of every stroke. The monitor can also give a heart rate in its display when Polar heart rate gear is used.

What this means to a paddler is that they can now measure their progress with real information not just race results. The monitor makes the adapter an analytical tool as well as a training tool. The adapter will help you identify your weak side. You can then paddle more strokes on that side to strengthen it. As you become familiar with the information supplied by the digital display monitor you will be able to find your most efficient heart rate range for any given distance at any given stroke output. This information can help to keep you from paddling too hard early on in a race, or from going too easy in the middle or late stages of a race. In general the adapter allows you to learn in detail about your paddling self, and the real beauty is the more you learn the greater your chances of improving!

The adapter to the Concept II Indoor Rower, presently set to be available for purchase later in 1996, will be manufactured and sold by Vermont Waterways Inc.

FOR ENQUIRIES CONTACT VERMONT WATERWAYS.

Vermont Waterways

Box 322 East Hardwick, Vermont, USA. Phone/Fax (802) 472 8271.

More Steering and More . . .

Illustrations in this chapter by unkown
artist, taken from a handout received at a seminar held at the University of Hawaii.

Jim Foti, winning steerer of the Lanikai Men's crew at the 1995 Moloka'i, one of the islands' most respected steerers and solo paddlers talks with Todd Bradley about regatta (flat water) and open ocean steering and more. RECORDED AT A UNIVERSITY OF HAWAII TWO-DAY SEMINAR.

Paddles, shafts, blades

Todd: This is a canoe sailing/surfing paddle I made based on the rudders used by the America's Cup Boat. I figured they had spent a lot of money in arriving at the eventual design, so why not try it.

The straight edge is the leading edge

and because the paddle is asymmetrical, you have to be careful when switching not to spin the paddle around as normal.

It has excellent bite and turning torque, whilst the trailing edge has minimum drag which in canoe sailing where you are poking most of the time, it works well. This paddle is perhaps a little small for six person canoe sailing and needs to be about a third larger – fine for surfing though.

Importantly a steering blade needs to be designed so as it "sticks" to the side of the hull. Ease of control with minimum effort. The raised curvature or dyhedral on the back of the blade creates areas of high and low pressure, like a wing, which helps to force the blade against the hull. This allows you to steer with one hand, the blade locked-in allowing you to extend the free arm over the ama side.

Jim: Sometimes also, a new blade can have all the right physical attributes, looking as if it should work, but because of the new varnish or epoxy coating you find it slips out on you. I like it when it wears a bit down to the wood, then it bites.

Todd: Because you are wedging the blade against the hull and "torquing" it, you need a strong paddle, a shaft that won't break on you. My shafts are two piece with a carbon laminate through the centre.

Now with the extra rocker of the Bradley and Force 5 canoes, I've designed my blades to be longer, without altering width. In amongst the waves the steerer is often very high out of the water. A shorter blade height is fine for flat water racing.

To minimize slippage, I wet sand the powerface straight up and down and I add rubberized tape at the neck of the paddle which really helps it grip.

Jim: Clubs have varying paddling styles which require different blade angles. In flat water races, the steerer needs to conform as closely as possible to the other five paddlers. If the guys are using ten degree shafts, then I might use seven, this allows me to be a little more in sync when I'm paddling.

In a distance race where you are poking more than paddling, there is less need to conform. As far as using bent shafts for steering, once again if its flat you can get away with it, but in the rough you're gonna want a straight shaft so as you can maximize your leverage and lean to the left as you poke on the right.

Regatta or sprint race starts

Jim: In regatta races, the steerer has a lot of responsibility and needs to take charge. You don't want a whole lot of shouting going on up the length of the canoe – take charge. If you also don't know what's going on – pretend you do! Better that someone does than no one. The crew has to have confidence in the steerer.

You have to know the course. Get the canoe on the line in plenty of time. You have to account for any cross winds and currents and begin figuring out how you're going to deal with it.

While waiting, it's best to keep the

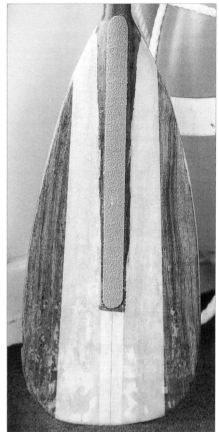

canoe into the wind nose or tail. Setting yourself up for a good start is crucial.

Todd: When you're at your lane, notice the flags either side of you. If you know you have a green flag as your marker and there's yellow and red either side, then that's the parameter within which you work.

For the return part of the course, before the race starts, look ninety degrees behind you and find a landmark to focus on, a building, a parked car a stationary cloud so as you know to aim for it if you lose sight of the marker.

It is easy to confuse which is your flag to aim for when there are similar (or same coloured flags) on the course. With your landmark you'll know if you're on track.

Paddle steering and poking

Jim: The steerer needs to tell the crew when to go and needs to be very vocal so as everyone hits at the same time.

The mechanics of good flat water paddling come into play for paddle steering. You will need to paddle steer as much as you can. A lot depends on the wind and how much it affects your direction.

If you want go left you poke to the left and the deal here is you are prying or pulling the back over to the right which brings the nose around to the left and vice-versa . You don't necessarily have to pry as such, you can just poke for subtle alteration and pry for a more dramatic response.

Alternatively in paddle steering you can pull the back of the canoe over to the left bringing the nose over to the right and again vice-versa. So, if the canoe is going slightly off course and the nose is swinging left, you can paddle steer by reaching out from the side of the canoe and pulling inwards with the blade to correct the direction without switching sides and poking on the right.

You want to be paddling as much as possible and keep as straight as possible, watching flags (using peripheral vision) and keeping in time with your crew.

With paddle steering you don't want to let the canoe move too far off course as it will require a lot of effort to correct it, which slows the canoe down. You have to anticipate and feel if the canoe is moving away on you and catch it early.

At the moment you sense the canoe drifting off, one or two angle paddle steering strokes will correct it – wind factor is always the problem.

If there's a strong cross wind, you're gonna kill yourself trying to paddle steer all the way. If you can correct the canoe quickly with one poke as opposed to taking six paddle strokes – do it.

PADDLE STEERING IS DEFINITELY A POWER MOVE. YOU HAVE TO BE STRONG AND EFFICIENT TO PULL IT OFF.

Turns, set up and uni

Jim: Setting up for the turn is the next hurdle. You line up your flag. The last thing you wanna do to yourself is go in too tight. You need to have a nice angle coming in and be taking your time. You need to be about half way over in your lane. When you're about twenty or thirty yards away you can start angling into it without killing the speed – you want as much speed as you can. You can pretty much paddle steer into the marker almost ninety degrees into the turn. Then execute your poke on the left and call your uni (*oo-nee*). Optimally you want to rub the marker on the third quarter of ama length.

YOU DON'T WANT TO OVERDO THE POKE SO AS YOU KILL THE CANOE'S SPEED – POKING TOO HARD TOO EARLY, TOO FAST. This will save your paddle from breaking by feathering it in and giving it a nice angle. Steerers break paddles because they've left it too late and they try turning the whole canoe in one huge poke!

Maintain the uni for three to five strokes depending on conditions. Rub on that third quarter of the ama, then release your uni. Hopefully you haven't killed too much speed before you're off again.

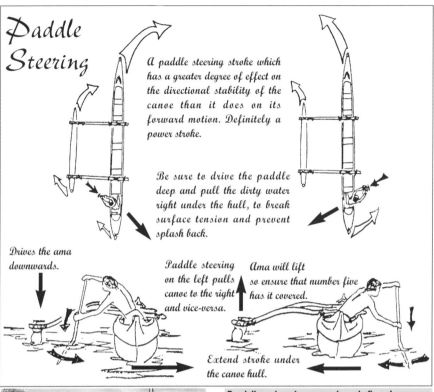

Paddle Steering

A paddle steering stroke which has a greater degree of effect on the directional stability of the canoe than it does on its forward motion. Definitely a power stroke.

Be sure to drive the paddle deep and pull the dirty water right under the hull, to break surface tension and prevent splash back.

Drives the ama downwards.

Paddle steering on the left pulls canoe to the right and vice-versa.

Ama will lift so ensure that number five has it covered.

Extend stroke under the canoe hull.

Jim Foti - demonstrating paddle steering

Paddle steering can be defined as any stroke which contributes to the forward motion and directional stability of the canoe.

The above shows a stroke not unlike a draw stroke. It is important when performing this stroke to try to bury the blade under the hull as much as possible so as to break the surface tension of the water and sweep the dirty water away.

If you stop your stroke short, the dirty water will bash up against the side of canoe hull and reflect back off causing turbulence and making the turning effect of your stroke inefficient.

Stroking like this on the right side endangers the ama - ensure that number five covers the ama. Not to be used in choppy or rough water!

Paddle Steering

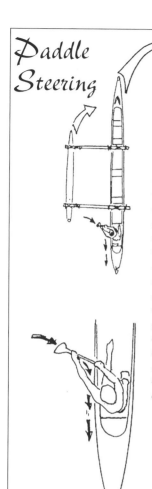

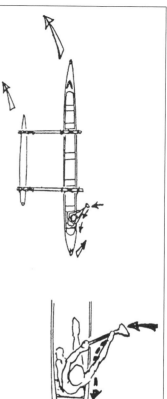

This paddle steering stroke provides the optimum balance between a forward stroke and a directional one. Now lets get one thing straight – this is not, repeat not, a J stroke (which has the stroke configuration in reverse order to this ie the stroke is initially made parallel to the hull then is swept away forming the tail of the J configuration). This can be thought of as more of a C stroke.

Be sure to perform this stroke as cleanly as possible to avoid splashback and undue turbulence against the hull. This stroke requires pure, raw strength to pull it off and a degree of finesse.

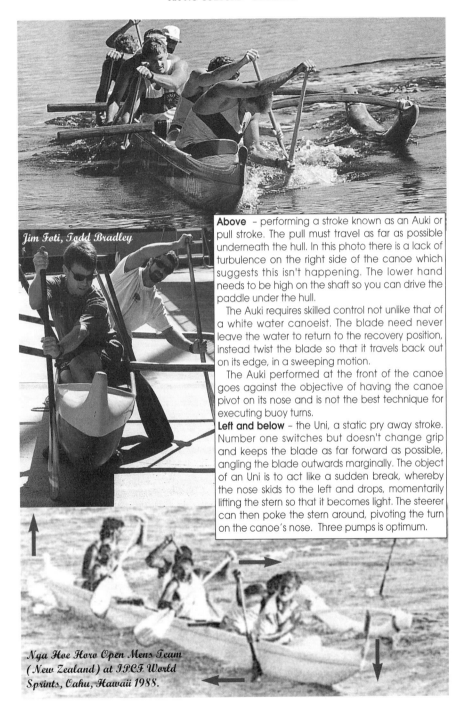

Jim Foti, Todd Bradley

Above - performing a stroke known as an Auki or pull stroke. The pull must travel as far as possible underneath the hull. In this photo there is a lack of turbulence on the right side of the canoe which suggests this isn't happening. The lower hand needs to be high on the shaft so you can drive the paddle under the hull.

The Auki requires skilled control not unlike that of a white water canoeist. The blade need never leave the water to return to the recovery position, instead twist the blade so that it travels back out on its edge, in a sweeping motion.

The Auki performed at the front of the canoe goes against the objective of having the canoe pivot on its nose and is not the best technique for executing buoy turns.

Left and below - the Uni, a static pry away stroke. Number one switches but doesn't change grip and keeps the blade as far forward as possible, angling the blade outwards marginally. The object of an Uni is to act like a sudden break, whereby the nose skids to the left and drops, momentarily lifting the stern so that it becomes light. The steerer can then poke the stern around, pivoting the turn on the canoe's nose. Three pumps is optimum.

Nga Hoe Horo Open Mens Team (New Zealand) at IPCF World Sprints, Oahu, Hawaii 1988.

Todd: The mechanics behind the uni are important to understand so as to make it work. The uni is called when the steerer at number six pokes their blade on the left side in the critical part of the turn and the stroke pokes an uni on the right.

Lots of practice is needed to pull off a good turn and all canoe types react differently according to the rocker line, length and tail shape – also the type of ama. You have to keep a wide berth as you are coming in with as much speed as you can when you call that uni. If when the steerer sets the poke and the number one sets their uni and there isn't enough hull speed, nothing's gonna happen. That's the point when excessive pumping starts because you know the canoe has stopped. So the key is to have as much speed as possible. THE UNI SHOULD LAST FOR ABOUT FOUR OR FIVE SECONDS AND ACCOUNT FOR A TWENTY DEGREE PORTION OF THE TURN ONLY.

WHAT HAPPENS WHEN YOU SET THE UNI, IS THAT YOU ARE STOPPING THE FRONT OF THE CANOE. THE FRONT DROPS AND THE TAIL LIFTS AND ITS CRITICAL THAT AT THAT MOMENT THE STEERER TIMES THEIR POKE, WHEN THE TAIL IS AT ITS LIGHTEST AND FREE TO SLIDE AROUND. THREE BIG UNI SHOULD ALLOW THE STEERER TO GET THE CANOE TO PIVOT AROUND ON THE NOSE. NOT THE TAIL – THE NOSE!

As the number one pumps the uni, the steerer a split second after each uni, pokes. So poke, uni, poke, uni, poke, uni. You don't want to hold the uni too long and not all the way around as the canoe's momentum will see it around the rest of the way – and you want to get paddling again as soon as possible.

Now you're also going to have to look around you and account for the other canoes in opposite lanes. Avoid conflict and collisions.

Jim: When the uni is being performed the crew can really back off on the power and just go through the motions – at this point you just want to pivot. Full power from the crew will kill it. Number two can paddle steer out on the left and also help to pull the nose around.

Paddle Control

Todd: When you paddle steer, it's important to drive the water under the hull. Otherwise the water just bounces off the hull and nothing happens. Choke up real high on the shaft, drive deep and pull under the hull to make it effective.

Also with the uni, you want to have the blade as far forward as you can so as the pivot point is also as far forward as possible. As long as you can keep it effective and not lose control.

Jim: It's also crucial to control the blade and not to have it slip away on you. Use your lower hand like an oarlock, partly on the gunwale, the shaft resting in your hand. This way you maintain paddle control.

Todd: And keep your paddle blade upright (or even tilted forwards slightly). It will respond and stick better. Keep it close to your body to maximize leverage. Don't angle it backwards, that just creates drag and is ineffective.

DISTANCE PADDLING

Poking – anticipation is the key

Todd: In distance steering, where steerers are staying in the canoe for long periods of time (two to six hours) the most crucial element for the steerer is to be efficient.

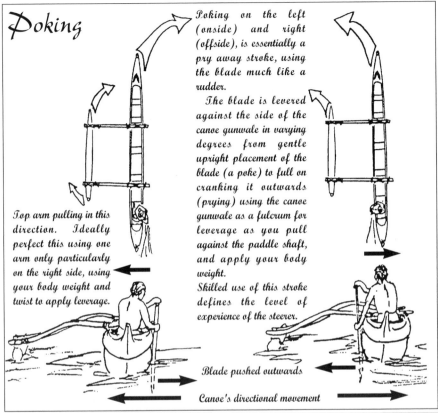

Poking

Poking on the left (onside) and right (offside), is essentially a pry away stroke, using the blade much like a rudder.

The blade is levered against the side of the canoe gunwale in varying degrees from gentle upright placement of the blade (a poke) to full on cranking it outwards (prying) using the canoe gunwale as a fulcrum for leverage as you pull against the paddle shaft, and apply your body weight.

Skilled use of this stroke defines the level of experience of the steerer.

Top arm pulling in this direction. Ideally perfect this using one arm only particularly on the right side, using your body weight and twist to apply leverage.

Blade pushed outwards

Canoe's directional movement

Developing a one-handed technique so that you can get your free arm over the ama side when poking on the right is essential to keep the ama down.

Once perfected it's a real buzz to plant the blade on this side and lean out on the left as the canoe surges down a swell It is the sort of sensation you get in pulling anything off well that requires an element of difficulty and with it the rewards of having your canoe running that fine line between being in control and on the verge of losing it! That's the reward a steerer feels - between control and walking the fine line.

A well designed blade that sticks to the side of the canoe hull is necessary for this. Confidence in your steering stick is crucial. One-handed steering also has the advantage of allowing you more freedom to rotate and look around you. Steering is undoubtedly an art that with time becomes more a matter of finesse and touch and less of brute strength.

Avoid lots of paddle steering as this will hurt you over a long period of time. A lot of poking is important and the pokes must be as minimal as possible. The reason for this is, that each time you poke, you're causing drag against the side of the canoe. Much like a caterpillar tractor which works by slowing down one tractor and keeping the other side driving to initiate the turn. But with this you create drag – your worst enemy – which you want to minimize.

IN ORDER TO MINIMIZE DRAG YOU NEED TO ANTICIPATE THE CANOE'S MOVEMENTS. THE CANOE CONSISTENTLY WANDERS AROUND WITH THE VARIABLES OF OCEAN MOVEMENTS, CURRENT, TIDES AND WINDS. THERE IS NO CENTERBOARD, JUST FORTY FOOT PLUS OF ROUNDED HULL.

So you have to stay focused on the whole hull of the canoe and feel how it's interacting with the ocean. If the canoe starts to run in a direction contrary to what you want, it will take a lot of drag to correct. It's important to be really in tune with the canoe and to catch any wandering early. Many steerers just don't want to talk or be distracted from focusing on the canoe, especially in rough water.

Jim: YEAH. YOU'VE GOT TO WIELD THAT PADDLE LIKE A GLADIATOR'S SWORD!

Finding the sweetspot

Todd That's right. Constantly switching left, right, left, right. Keeping the canoe on track. Lose it in the rough and you'll kill the hull speed then have to rescue it radically.

THERE'S NOT A LOT OF PADDLE STEERING IN DISTANCE RACING. YOU'RE WAY BETTER LETTING YOUR ENGINES DO THE PULLING AND FOCUSING ON SETTING THE CANOE UP ON THE SWEETSPOT – EVERY CANOE HAS ONE, WHERE IT FITS INTO A WAVE AND GOES OFF!

The steerer has to have their radar constantly switched on – looking for that zone in which the canoe is going to maximise hull speed. The steerer needs to work a path amongst the waves and swells

Todd Bradley wielding his paddle like a gladiator's sword. The most dynamic image of a steerer you are liable to see in a long while. For those who think it's a picnic back there - get a life!
Photo provided by
Todd Bradley

keeping the sweetspot for as long as they can. You can really wander around looking for ocean that works for you, not against you. You find it. You loose it. Go looking again and so on.

ANTICIPATE AND CORRECT BEFORE IT HAPPENS. AVOID DRAG AND ALL THE ENERGY WASTED TRYING TO GET THE CANOE BACK ON COURSE. ANTICIPATION IS EVERYTHING!

You're a rudder not a motor

Jim: Of course you sneak in paddle strokes when you can – the canoe's running and on track. But don't get into that mind set "I've gotta paddle! I've gotta be a motor!" You'll lose focus looking for and staying on that sweet spot.

IF YOU'RE TRYING TO PADDLE TOO MUCH, YOU'RE NOT FOCUSING ON STEERING ENOUGH. THAT'S YOUR JOB. DON'T FORGET THAT. NO ONE ELSE IS GONNA DO IT FOR YOU.

New generation canoes

Todd: The new designs (Force 5 and Bradley) are presenting some challenges for steerers. It was interesting at the Moloka'i race this year. We knew it was going to be rough – it was gonna be big, – and there were a lot of people who had never paddled a Force 5 in rough water who assumed that it would be more user friendly than the Bradley Jim was using with Lanikai.

In comparison, if the Hawaiian Class Racer is say three on a scale of one to ten in terms of ease of steering and controlability, the Bradley would be up around seven and the Force 5 a six. That's all there is in it – about ten percent difference in terms of degree of looseness and difficulty steering in the rough. The Force 5 holds a slightly better line having marginally less rocker

than the Bradley.

What was interesting after the race was competitors were then saying that the Force 5 was here . . . it was there . . . it was all over the place. Well of course it was. It's a Porche – like the Bradley is! But not quite as lively. It is a "bear" to steer in the rough. You've gotta stay on top of it. Jim in the Bradley had to be ten percent more focused than I had to be in the Force 5. That being said, if you learn to tame it and use the ocean, then you can fly!

Your anticipation has to be twice as fast. These canoes react almost instantly – no delay like in the Hawaiian Class Racer. THOSE WHO THOUGHT THE NEW DESIGNS WERE GOING TO BE A CARPET RIDE HAD A RUDE AWAKENING. STEERING ONE IS A HARD GRIND, BUT NOT WITHOUT REWARDS. NOW THAT THERE WILL BE A GRADUAL MOVEMENT TO THESE HULLS FOR DISTANCE OCEAN RACING, STEERERS ARE GOING TO GO THROUGH A NEW LEARNING CURVE.

Riding the new hulls on a wave, they have a lot of rocker and ride the wave at different points. The Bradley rides at about four seat and the Force 5 just behind the iako. About a four foot margin of difference – this is the sweetspot.

Catching runners

Jim: When you're out on the ocean everything's moving around you – behind, in front and to the sides. You're looking for the troughs in front, looking to set the nose in a downwards incline, following the bump ahead of you.

Todd: PROBABLY THE BEST TRAINING FOR A STEERER IN LEARNING OCEAN DYNAMICS IS PADDLING IN A SOLO OUTRIGGER CANOE.

Jim: Or a kayak.

In this sequence, note how the steerer keeps weight over the centre of the canoe. The free arm across the body, the other tucked in close. One hand on the shaft, twisting the body to apply leverage against the underside of the canoe hull.

Moments later the free arm goes over the ama side and number five leans farther out to stabilize the ama. Intense concentration and a delicate touch are needed here. Number five is often referred to as the "keeper" of the ama – working together with the steerer to prevent a huli.

Ama! Outrigger Canoe Club off Barbers Point Oahu, doing the ama fandango! Quick reactions save the canoe on this occasion. Steerer pokes on the right, a momentary lapse of concentration frees the ame and physics does the rest. Both steerer and number five have to work together constantly to keep the ama down – eye-balling its travel through the water. If they lose it, then it's a good idea if the rest o the crew pitch in.

Todd: Remember that with a forty feet plus hull, you're not going to ride the swells straight down the face. You're always going to ride down sideways so as you can fit the canoe length on the face. Otherwise you're just going to stuff the manu into the trough, lose speed and have the wave overtake you.

When you're riding a bumps out in the ocean one thing that has to be learned is that the wave or bump that comes up behind you is not necessarily the one that's going to be your ticket. It's the one you don't see starting to form.

You are feeling for the wave that's embryonic. You want to put the canoe in that area – where it is forming. Don't kill your crew trying to catch something unrideable or not worth it relative to the energy they expended in trying to catch an already dead wave.

A good example of number five and number six working together to save the ama. Steerer is poking or the right and five has come across on the same side as four. A close working relationship needs to b fostered between steerer and five who should ideally have steering knowledge. Kia Opua OCC Moloka'i 1995.

In this sequence, where the turn is a ninety degree angle around a turn buoy on a marathon course, the steerer has moved the top hand just above mid way on the shaft for better blade control. This allows the body to have a lower centre of gravity and therefore more effective lean into the turn and application of body weight to the shaft.

The first frame shows the turn being initiated with blade swept back. The expression shows full concentration and commitment to executing the turn at precisely the right moment. In the second frame the blade is swung forward, steerer leans over the gunwale while applying full weight to the shaft

Judgement as to when to initiate the turn and then fully commit to it in the second phase, is largely a question of experience. There are a host of other factors which the experienced steerer needs to consider: wave and swell action, wind and current, are all crucial elements which can either hinder or assist the turn. There are very few constants in an open ocean environment.

Jim: REMEMBER YOU ARE NOT SO MUCH LOOKING FOR WAVES, YOU'RE FEELING FOR THEM – IN YOUR BUTT. WITH YOUR INSTINCT.

Todd: You'll notice the ocean flatten out ahead of you. Then you start feeling – anticipating. The ocean begins to rip or tear open and a wave or swell is about to be born. That is where you want to put the canoe. This comes with experience and time on solo canoe or kayaks. Seeing the flat spot that's about to tear open.

IT IS IMPORTANT TO SHARE THIS KNOWLEDGE WITH JUNIOR PADDLERS. TEACH THEM EARLY TO GET THEM INTO NEW HABITS.

Steerers will often bob in time with the crew's rhythm when poking. This is to stay in time with their stroke rate so if you do take a stroke it is automatically in sync without having to adjust. In this way the steerer is always ready to take a stroke in rhythm with the crew.

ONE IMPORTANT THING TO CONSIDER IN CREW SELECTION FOR ROUGH WATER DISTANCE, IS TO SELECT A NUMBER FIVE WHO HAS STEERING KNOWLEDGE. THAT IS YOUR HELPER – HELPING TO PROTECT THE AMA.

There are many times when the canoe starts running left and the steerer is locked in trying to stop the runaway. In most cases (with the new designs at any rate) you can stop it, but only with a serious poke to the right, which puts your ama at risk. That's where your five seat comes into action.

They have to know instinctively that when the canoe runs left, you're gonna poke on the right. At that point, five seat has gotta go out on the left; holding the ama down; switching sides and paddle steering. Pulling the nose around. They must have steering knowledge.

I have guys like Marc Haine, Walter Guild and Bruce Black who steer canoes and surf and they know when I'm in trouble. I don't have to say a thing and they're on it. But I don't have to be in trouble, they will just do it anyway. That way, one through four can just focus on paddling. So the steerer and number five work as a team.

Staying hydrated and fueled up

Jim: IN DISTANCE STEERING YOU HAVE TO MAKE SURE YOU'RE HYDRATED PROPERLY. IT'S EASY, BEING CAUGHT UP IN IT ALL, TO FORGET TO DRINK. IF YOU GET THIRSTY AFTER AN HOUR IT'S TOO LATE. YOU'VE GOTTA AVOID GETTING THIRSTY – IF YOU ARE THIRSTY YOU ARE DEHYDRATED!

Have a Camelbak (or water bottle with a tube attached) in the canoe; or have the support boat supply you with water every twenty minutes. It's important to be strong the whole way. Set yourself up a smorgasbord of carbo goodies at the back.

Todd: At the Hawaiki-Nui race in Tahiti, Jim and I were setting up our six seat with Powerbars and everything else and the other guys were asking "what'ya doing?" We had to remind them that we were paddling iron.

I have a cup with a hook that has my bars and goodies in it. Jim uses tape, – but he'll probably use a cup now! So hydrate often and regularly, Eat occasionally.

Change-overs

Todd: You can see a drop is going to be made – the coach usually decides this – and you see the support boat screams off ahead. The steerer maintains the intended course and when you are ready, wave your paddle to tell the change-over paddlers to get into the water spacing themselves apart.

Mooloolaba Masters –
Hamilton Cup Australia '95.

One of a steerer's biggest challenges is positioning the canoe to make a pick-up. Full concentration is paramount to avoid running over the swimmers or missing them altogether. Sharp eyes and good reflexes are needed and an understanding of how the canoe responds to the paddlers exiting and entering.

Here Todd adopts a powerful grasp on the paddle shaft, blade upright to keep the canoe straight. Just before the paddlers are in he's paddling to help get canoe speed up.

Keeping the canoe dry

You want to keep the canoe as dry as possible, so unzipping for change-overs is left until the last possible minute with the process beginning at the back of the canoe moving forwards.

If it is a one-three-five change, the steerer calls "five zip". Five unzips – three knows they're next. Now five's paddling so call "three zip".

One and two will wait until the absolute last minute as this is where the most water comes in. They have to unzip, get the paddle in a holder and bale out – fast. This may take twenty or ten yards depending on the paddler's abilities.

The same with zipping up. When one or two gets in, they zip up first whilst those behind start paddling. When one and two start paddling then three knows it's time to zip up. Three stops and starts – then five.

Jim: If it's really rough, then you'll tend to have them all zip up as soon as their butts hit the seat,

WATER IN THE CANOE IS A KILLER AND THE PADDLERS SHOULD KNOW WHETHER TO PADDLE OR ZIP UP – WHICH ONE IS MORE IMPORTANT IS DICTATED BY CONDITIONS. THEY SHOULD ALSO KNOW WHEN TO BAIL WITHOUT HAVING TO BE ASKED BY THE STEERER AND UNZIP WHEN THE TIME IS RIGHT.

Todd: WATER IS YOUR WORST ENEMY. IT IS BEST TO STOP AND BAIL WHEN THERE IS A SMALL AMOUNT OF WATER IN THE CANOE. NOT WAIT FOR HEAPS. BETTER THAT THEY ARE BAILING FOR ONLY HALF A CHANGE RATHER THAN TWO. IF FOUR SEAT HAS WATER, THEN BAIL. BY THE TIME SIX HAS WATER, YOU'VE GOT WAY TOO MUCH.

Who gets in and paddling first adds some spice to the task. OCC Kona Coast.

Hamilton Cup. Mooloolaba Masters one, two and four change. Relief paddlers in correct order in the water and making themselves visible in the choppy sea.

You only get one chance! Pulling yourself in as smoothly as possible is essential. This is hard core stuff in rough water. A bruised body is all part of the trade off!

Tiot Canoe Ceremony

Whilst on Catalina Island the Catalina outrigger race coincided with the launching of a traditional Tiot canoe as used by Native American Indians of the region.

Made from redwood planks lashed together much like the canoes of Oceania and decorated with abalone shell these wide-beamed cargo canoes (dry weight of five hundred pounds) were used for trading soapstone and deer between the mainland and Catalina and along the mainland coast by the Tongua people (called Gabrieleno by the Spanish) of the region.

Canoe Culture in action which Ka'nu Culture, the book, supports absolutely!

The canoe was named "Moomat Ahiko" – "Breath of the Ocean".

For further details: TIOT SOCIETY Cindi Alvitri, PO Box 1138, Avalon, Ca USA 90704. Tel: 310–510 9571

Koa Culture, Koa Ritual.

Without doubt, one of the highlights of my three trips to Hawaii during 1995, was taking part in a Koa canoe blessing ceremony on the Big Island of Hawaii. It represented the chance for me to attend something unique, powerful and moving.

Far from being an everyday occurrence, if you should ever have the opportunity to share in such a ceremony, it will open your eyes and your heart to a better understanding of Polynesian spiritual attachment to the canoe.

Attending such a ceremony should be part of a pilgrimage, something which could perhaps be seen as being as important as paddling Moloka'i. It is not until you have savoured everything linked with the outrigger canoe that you can say you fully understand what outrigger canoe racing is all about.

KEAUHOU
KONA, HAWAII

KEAUHOU CANOE CLUB

P.O. Box 390755, Keauhou-Kona, Hawaii 96739,   Phone :

The Board of Directors & Members of Keauhou CC & Malama Ula CC invite your participation at the commencement of shaping of our twin koa racing canoes on

Monday, September 5, 1995
at Keauhou CC's Halau Wa'a, Keauhou Bay.

The Canoes will be shaped by na kalaiwa'a o Kona

Bill Rosehill & Jerry Benson

A sunrise Blessing ceremony will be officiated by Kahu Kaniela Akaka

Our ceremony will start at 5.45 am.
Your arrival by 5.30 am is respectfully requested.
A club Celebration will follow. Please allow two hours.

89

*W*hilst on the Big Island of Hawaii for the Queen Liliuokalani race in early September, race director Mike Atwood, a long time paddler and one of the sport's true gentlemen, showed me much that I needed to see.

Within minutes of our meeting, he mentioned (as if where more important than the race itself) that on the Monday following the race, a *Koa* canoe blessing ceremony was to be held at his club, Keauhou.

Having read about such traditions, I immediately recognized the significance of this invitation. The ritual blessing of Koa canoes is intrinsic to their production and to the culture of the Polynesians.

Mike told me how the Keauhou club had acquired a log which, when split in two, was large enough to carve two canoes. For ten years the log had been waiting – drying and curing. If carved too early it could split as it continued to dry out. Now, the time was right.

One of the new canoes was destined for the Malama Ula club of Maui, the other to remain on the Big Island with the Keauhou club. The canoes when complete, will be considered as sister canoes and whenever there is a double-hull race, these two will be joined together once more.

At 4.30am on Monday September 5, I found myself standing on the dew sodden grass in front of the club's *halau wa'a* (canoe house) still recovering from the weekend's big events. In the pitch dark, cars began arriving and people shuffled in from the darkness.

Casual yet solemn introductions were made. I sensed the collective consciousness of the people who were coming together to celebrate an ancient ritual. A gathering of like-minded people who acknowledged the significance of this tradition.

Finally the *Kahu*, his wife and children arrived. They had brought with them sacred *Ti-leaves* (used throughout Polynesia as a bringer of good fortune) which she began to tear into strips. A large *Koa* bowl was also filled, with water from two separate containers.

Meanwhile preparations were underway for breakfast which was to follow. A celebration was also at hand.

Kahu Kaniela Akaka, who conducted the sunrise blessing ceremony, holding a koa bowl in which was mixed fresh and ocean water brought from the vicinity where the living tree had been found.

By now the sky had become quite bright and everything was in its place. The *Kahu* assumed his role and asked us to form a semi-circle facing the mountain. He explained: *The significance of the canoe blessing ceremony taking place at sunrise is to appease the god Ku (one of the four major gods of the Hawaiian people) and to signify and support the event as the bringer of life, as sunrise is a symbol of birth and creation. Likewise the making of Koa canoe, is indeed a process which involves the metamorphosis, the birth of a new creation at the hands of the Kalaiwa'a (canoe builder).*

Another important time of day to the Hawaiians, a time of ritual and ceremony, was mid-day. At this time the sun is at its highest and no shadow is cast and it was believed your Mana or spirit is strongest when your shadow receded into your head – a very sacred part of your body.

The Hawaiian belief (like other indigenous people world-wide) was that life is pervaded by supernatural powers which were personified into gods of nature. There were many such gods worshiped and praised, but at times neglected, leading to certain natural disasters. To appease the gods, the Hawaiians offered ritual and

The two hewn logs ready for blessing at either side of a completed Koa canoe, sheltered in the halau wa'a (canoe house) of the Keauhou Canoe Club. From one massive single Koa tree, the trunk was cut in half and then partially shaped or hewn therefore providing the foundation of the two Ka'ele (hulls). Logs of this size are rarely found today. This log is ten years old, very well cured and ready for the Kalaiwa'a O Kona (canoe builders of Kona) Bill Rosehill and Jerry Brown to begin work.

ceremony to ensure that whatever was being undertaken would be successful. So that in all aspects of life there was prayer and ceremony.

The ceremony this morning is called WaiKai (water blessing) and it is important that during the ceremony those present free themselves of any negative emotions – to think only positive thoughts. This is important because the collective Mana of all present will be imparted to the canoes. Our life force being given to the canoes.

Leonard "Bully" Kapahulehua of the Malama Ula club of Maui, performed a powerful and moving haka in expressing his club's feelings about being one of the recipients of the new Koa canoes.

Before we begin the ceremony I would ask for any of those amongst us to step forward and speak to clear your thoughts of anything which you would like to share with us, as to what you would like to see happen with these canoes.

At this point, various members of those gathered stepped forward, introduced themselves and then spoke to us –

"We are today moving into the future whilst preserving the past. Combining the knowledge of the past. Perpetuating something that was done in Polynesia, northern parts of America and other parts of the world, that is still being done – maybe with new concepts and techniques, but with the same ideas that were used many, many years ago, and were practiced as a very important part of life."

"What is wonderful about all of this is that it also started another program in re-generating a Koa forest from which this log came. Today if you go up and look at where this log came from, you will find literally thousands of young Koa trees coming up in the area where the cattle have been removed and the Koa have been left to grow, freely."

"The exciting thing about this is that it is a rebirth, a rebirth of these logs as they are entering a new life. It is a very spiritual thing for me to see that a tree is not one living organism, but it is like a club, it is part of a system of living organisms which create a whole. It is wonderful to have watched the Koa sit here and wait, in the same way that this club has sat here and waited, for the right time for the sprouting and germination of the new seed, which is symbolic of the hillside upon which the new Koa are growing."

Club representatives of Keauhou Canoe Club (Hawaii) and Malama Ula (Maui) with Kahu Kaniela Akaka and the Kalaiwa'a Wa'a O Kona, Bill Rosehill and Jerry Brown after the ceremony.

Following these comments, Leonard *Bully* Kapahulehua of the Malama Ula club of Maui introduced himself.

My name is Bully Kapahulehua. We, the Malama Ula Club of Maui, are very thankful for this opportunity to join the Keauhou ohana (Keauhou family), Mr Greenwell and the ohana here from Keauhou. Mahalo to you all for giving us this opportunity to be with you and to have this Koa wa'a made here. Mahalo nui loa.

Whereupon he went straight from talking into a powerful and moving *haka,* which pierced the morning stillness and cut right to the heart with its powerful sound and imagery of the ancestors and a time gone by. It took us all by surprise, transfixed us and made us acutely aware of the emotional and spiritual value placed in this event. I was experiencing culture shock. Wishing I was Polynesian, I couldn't help but feel clumsy in my Anglo-Saxon skin and even more uncomfortable about my own culture's historical dealings with the Polynesian peoples.

My name is Alika Atay and I'm from the Malama Ula Club on Maui. We're very proud that, in what is a very challenging time for us, we run a youth program in summer time which we call, Na Keiki O Ke Kai, Children of the Sea. We primarily focus on outrigger canoeing and in addition to this we do surfing, fishing and everything to do with the sea.

It is very exciting for us to be a part of this. In the summer program we take our kids at least one day a week into the mountains to get them away from the sea. But the ocean is our primary focus and we are very excited about seeing the completion of our canoe and to have it visit all the waters of the islands.

By now the purpose of the ceremony was cemented in all present. Powerful, emotional words had reached us and we were in no doubt as to the purpose and significance of our gathering together.

Kahu Kaniela Akaka then explained the contents of the Koa bowl. It contained a mixture of both fresh and salt water. The fresh water had been gathered from a stream that had run beside the living tree, and the salt water from the ocean at the base of the mountain where the tree had stood. The fresh water had fed the tree during its lifetime and the ocean was to be its final destiny – rebirth as a canoe.

Facing the mountain we began a *mele* (chant) which continued for some ten minutes, repetitively and to a point of mild hypnosis. When the sun appeared as a yellow brilliant orb above the mountain the *mele* ceased.

The *Kahu* then continued a *mele* followed with Hawaiian words, where he talked much about the koa. He then walked around the semi-circle of some forty-five

people and sprinkled each one of us with the sacred water by dipping *Ti-leaves* into the bowl before brushing them over our heads and torsos, all the time chanting.

Once he had completed the semi-circle of people, he moved to the *halau* and blessed not only the two awaiting hulls, but also the ground upon which they rested. Then the *halau* itself, all the time chanting and sprinkling sacred water. Finally moving back to the centre where he drank the remaining contents of the bowl.

It occurred to me how it is in life that we come across strange ironies. In the case of the *Koa* tree and therefore the *Koa* canoe, outrigger canoe racing, whilst reawakening a culture, has also highlighted the need to not only preserve the *Koa* tree but to foster its re-forestation. Of all the excuses, commercial or otherwise, for the felling of mature trees, the need to perpetuate a culture through the carving of canoes, is surely the most valid.

With the ceremony over in about forty-five minutes, gas burners were lit and woks were stirred into action as scrambled eggs, rice and sausages where prepared with hot coffee served.

The sun had fully risen and the ocean appeared glassy and peaceful. Optimism pervaded and even the birds seemed to have joined the celebration for the new life which had been born. I felt a deep happiness and gratitude for being a part of the ritual and of this magnificent sport, which has a real soul and a depth for any of those prepared to look for it.

Following are images of Koa canoes and accessories. A tribute to the masterful maritime woodcarving architects who create them. We must be grateful to them and to nature for providing the raw materials.

There are paddlers who will paddle only Koa constructed canoes. Their organic origins and their traditional associations and values being paramount to the paddler's personal beliefs.

As proud as this Koa once stood majestic and powerful on its mountain slopes, its leaves and branches touched by cool, fragrant mountain air, so now it is majestic and awesome as a seafaring craft. This magnificent Koa canoe owned by the Kailua Kona Club, Kai E Hitu (the last wave) was built by Tahitian master canoe builders from a massive single log, with little or no additional planking. The canoe, Heipualani, is the club's pride and joy. Invested in it is their heritage, their pride and their wealth.

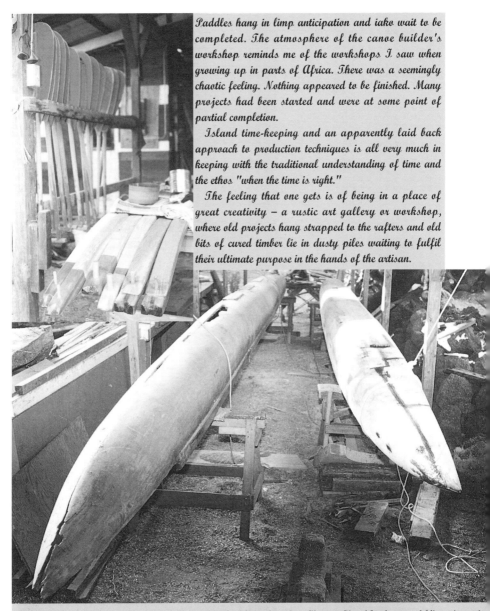

Paddles hang in limp anticipation and iako wait to be completed. The atmosphere of the canoe builder's workshop reminds me of the workshops I saw when growing up in parts of Africa. There was a seemingly chaotic feeling. Nothing appeared to be finished. Many projects had been started and were at some point of partial completion.

Island time-keeping and an apparently laid back approach to production techniques is all very much in keeping with the traditional understanding of time and the ethos "when the time is right."

The feeling that one gets is of being in a place of great creativity – a rustic art gallery or workshop, where old projects hang strapped to the rafters and old bits of cured timber lie in dusty piles waiting to fulfil their ultimate purpose in the hands of the artisan.

The workshop of Manny Veincent – Koa canoe builder – based at Kawai Hai (Gathering of Water) on the Big Island of Hawaii. Broken canoes in need of repair. In the hands of the canoe builders these canoes are carefully and lovingly restored to health with strips of Koa planking replacing the holes and cracks. The smell of timber mixed with ocean air pervades the atmosphere. Wood chips lie thick on the ground mixed with dust and sand. And all around the sound of insects, birds and trees whispering in the sea breeze.

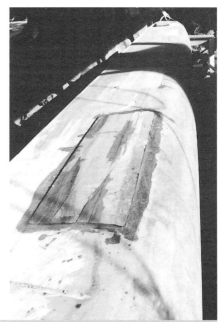

Smashed in bad weather, the canoe builder begins to restore the canoe to its former glory. Over time many a Koa canoe is transformed from a once near perfect log to a patchwork of laminations that have been added over time to repair damage.

A hewn log transforms into the Kino or Kuamo'o (hull). Traditionally much of this initial stage of hewing was carried out on the site where the tree was felled due naturally to its massive size. It was often left to cure there also. Finally it was hauled down the mountain slopes stern first, restrained by ropes and the strongest of men. This could take many days even months.

Prior to this event the Kahuna Kalai Wa'a performed a ceremony, Pui i Ka Wa'a, praying to protect the hull as it was hauled down the rugged mountainside. Once at the Halau Wa'a, either further curing would be done, or work on the hull would begin

Whilst a log forms the basis of the hull and part of the canoe sides, these are often built up using a series of Koa planks to achieve the desirable freeboard.

Shaped and polished – graceful curvatures such as this give Koa canoes individual character and grace, personality and charm uniquely their own. Koa canoe Kailua Kona, Queen Liliuokalani Race 1995. Below one of only three such Koa topsided canoes in California. The winged design surely a Native American Indian influence. Catalina 1995.

Hanging from the corrugated iron roof of Manny Veincent's workshop, a variety of ama for both paddled craft and sailing canoes. A mast and sail and lengths of Hau (Sea Hibiscus) cut, treated and dried ready to be made into iako.

The use of Hau iako and ama made from Wili'Wili completes the organic canoe. Increasing numbers of clubs are using Hau iako with their fiberglass canoes. Not only is it traditional but it makes excellent iako superior to laminated pine. Hau is lighter in weight, adds character to the rigging and because of the round profile is extremely strong.

Hau iako are not cheap. How does $US700 grab you for one! To obtain them a trip to the mangroves is required. The right tree branches with suitable curvature are selected and removed. Then in order to ensure they are free from borers they are soaked in the ocean for up to two weeks, before having the bark stripped and being allowed to fully dry out. The salt crystallization which occurs during the drying out process further prevents any infestation. Finally they are sanded and sealed with a lacquer.

Traditionally Hau was also used to make fishing net floats as the inner fibers are extremely fibrous with added strength and a degree of spring. These fibers were beaten and made into ropes and cords and in certain parts of the Pacific (Samoa, Fiji) were beaten to make Tapa or bark cloth and skirts.

It grows in lowland Hawaii and throughout the tropics. Called Fau in Samoa and Pago in Guam and Marianas. It is a small evergreen tree from 13-33 feet (4-10m) with a trunk up to six inches in diameter.

Hawaiian teams like to take their favourite set of Hau (Sea Hibiscus) iako with them, and why not, after all they're easy enough to manage.

Hau has also been used to make strong, lightweight iako for solo canoes by laminating strips of the wood together. Lightweight paddles can also be made, by the usual laminating techniques. However Hau is hard to come by and not readily available therefore items tend to be one-offs.

Tahitians make paddles from various mangrove trees, some of which have a greenish tinge. Hau – a fabulous natural timber which is ideally suited for iako and the perfect companion with a Koa canoe and an ama made from laminated Wili'Wili.

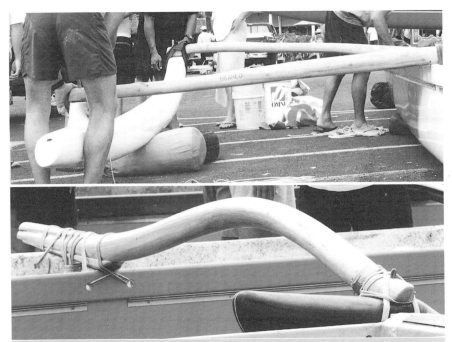

Nature's curvature; beautiful in form, perfect in function. The Hau's natural curvature makes for a seductive art form that would surely appeal to the collector of woodcarvings.

Traditional fishing canoe at Honaunau Bay, Big Island Hawaii – one of the island's many sacred sights. The Malia (the first fibreglass production canoe) originated from this Kona Coast region of the Big Island and you can see a basic similarity in design with this fishing canoe.

Ka'nu Culture Hats & Shirts.

ORDER FORM AT BACK OF BOOK.

KA'NU CULTURE TORSO WEAR

Time to grow up and break away from those big brash screened T's that keep you looking like an ageing hippy. Get entry into bars and restaurants with our deluxe embroidered polo shirt or kick back in our stylish T's. Choice of royal or navy blue, with gold and turquoise embroidery. Outrigger wear with a difference.

100% Cotton. Sizes L and XL.

T's $20 (Aust) Polo $28 (Aust)

KA'NU CULTURE HEAD GEAR

Aerodynamically streamlined, fully adjustable velcro strapping, available in royal or navy blue with gold and turquoise embroidery. Quick drying, lightweight Taslon. Keeps the sun out of your eyes, off your nose, minimizes cranial skin cancer and cerebral meltdown, tames long hair and gives bald paddlers added sex appeal. An absolute "must have" outrigging accessory.

One size fits all $15 (Aust)

KA'NU CULTURE PATCHES

High quality cotton patches provide you the freedom to have them easily sewn onto any garment, paddle bag or kit bag. 9.5cm X 5.0cm (3.7" x 2"). Gold and turquoise embroidery on navy blue background.
$8 (Aust)

Aotearoa
"Land of the Long White Cloud"

Waka Ama in New Zealand

Waka Te Te (fishing canoe) forty feet long and up to twenty paddlers.

The Legend of Maui

Maui was the youngest of five brothers. His father Makea-tu-tara, a minor god, was descended from Tama-nui-ki-te Rangi, an important member of a group of Polynesian gods His mother Taranga, was an earthwoman of the underworld.

Maui, prematurely born, was abandoned, as was sometimes customary but survived through the intervention of a divine ancestor who raised him and taught him supernatural ways.

In time, Maui returned to his family, whereupon he became his mothers favourite son and the ringleader of all manner of misadventure.

His natural sense of adventure and curiosity lead him to follow his mother into the underworld where he was introduced to his ancestress, Muriranga, who gave him a magic jawbone.

One day, his brothers prepared for a fishing trip but decided to leave Maui behind because they feared his supernatural powers.

Ever the adventurer, Maui stowed away on the canoe and when far from land he decided to try fishing for himself. Having no hook, he baited his magical jawbone and cast it over.

Immediately he hauled up the largest fish ever caught, Te-Ika-a-Maui (The Great Fish of Maui). This it is said, was the North Island of New Zealand. As Maui pulled, the North Island came up under the canoe and raised it high into the air on top of Mount Hikurangi, where a canoe's rocky outline remains today.

Maui's hook is said to be still embedded in the fish he caught and is seen on the southern extremity of Hawke's Bay.

Some southern Maori groups believe that Maui's canoe, Te Whaka-a-Maui, became the South Island, while Stewart Island is its anchor stone. Essentially the legend of Maui has been adopted by Maori of both the North and South Islands.

The Legend of Kupe

The unlikely discovery of the islands of Aotearoa, being so far south and remote, is symbolised in the Maori traditional legend of Kupe who is presumed to have discovered the islands around a thousand years ago, in the vicinity of 900 AD.

Kupe was a fisherman and seafarer from the island of Raiatea of the Society Islands, known in Maori legend as Hawaiki.

During his fishing trips, his bait and lure were regularly taken by a shoal of octopus, lead by a giant called Wheke-a-Muturangi (The Edge of the Horizon).

Enraged by this, Kupe chased the octopus, "the edge of the horizon" until he reached Aotearoa in his canoe, named Mata-Whao-rua, a distance of some two thousand four hundred miles. A fight insued, in which Kupe slayed the giant octopus in Cook Strait.

Before returning to his home, he named the country Aotea Roa "Land of the Long White Cloud", so impressed by the mountainous terrain and the clouds which shrouded them. After sailing carefully around the islands, he returned to tell of his discovery.

The tentacles of Wheke-a-Muturangi are said to signify not only the reaching out from Hawai'ki to other islands but also the length of the journey to Aotearoa.

Over the next five hundred years, legends tell of Kupe's journey being retraced by some thirty canoes using the traditional Polynesian seafaring skills of wave and star path navigation, setting a course "to the left of the setting sun in November . . ."

The journey began in Hawai'ki in waka. Our people built waka for getting people from one place to another, and sometimes this took great courage to achieve. These were prodigious journeys of the mind, of the spirit, and of the body.

Haare Williams JP, BA, Dip Ed 1990

For the Tangata Whenua - the people of the land of Aotearoa, the Maori - the paddle symbolizes a sense of purpose and direction whilst also affirming their close cultural links with the canoe. All individual Maori ancestry is intrinsically linked with a particular canoe upon which their forebears arrived on the shores of Aotearoa. This provides each person with an essential link back to Hawaiki - and beyond to creation itself.

Every beginning has its origins and I suppose every origin has its beginnings. In nearly all examples of human endeavour it takes special individuals to act as catalysts – to go beyond the dreamstate to actually manifest ideas into the realm of reality.

Not only does it take special individuals but often a special place, a power place, which contains within its boundaries or isolation an energy and predisposition to making it all happen.

Kris Kjeldsen strikes me as one of these catalysts and the northern New Zealand town of Pawarenga as one of those places. Although its population is predominantly Maori, the local Pawarenga community is a racial mix of Samoan, Pakeha and Rarotongan. Today, some eighty percent of this community are involved in some way with the sport of outrigger canoeing – or waka ama, its traditional name. As Anna Pospisil, co-ordinator of the Pawarenga Community Trust says, "Canoeing has brought a whole new focus and motivation to the community."

Kris Kjeldsen writes about the development of waka ama in Aotearoa.

Being one of the *elders* of outrigger canoe paddling in New Zealand and one of the three people responsible for a revival of the sport here, this is our story of the history and growth of waka ama in Aotearoa.

Waka ama (*outrigger canoe*) paddling was re-introduced in 1985 with the arrival of the *Hawaiki Nui*, the replica Polynesian voyaging canoe built and sailed by Matahi Whakataka (*master builder*) Brightwell on an epic voyage from Tahiti to Aotearoa.

Matahi spent four years in Tahiti

The Hawaiki Nui Tahiti 1984.
The arrival of this vessel from the place of origin
of the Maori, acted as a catalyst for the rekindling
of many traditional activities in Aotearoa - from
woodcarving to song and dance and waka ama.

building the *Hawaiiki Nui*, during which time he became involved in outrigger canoe racing, the national sport of Tahiti. He recognized that this would be the very thing to help the youth of New Zealand regain some of their cultural heritage and traditions.

Before settling in New Zealand, I had paddled for Kai Nalu Canoe Club in Southern California and was also involved for a short time in Hawaii. So when I finally settled in the small Maori village of Pawarenga in the far north of the North Island on the edge of Whangape Harbour, (where I was to live for about fifteen years) I wondered why there was no traditional Maori canoe racing.

On reading in the newspaper about Matahi's intended voyage and his dream to rekindle racing of traditional canoes, I knew it was time to do something about it and so I was on the beach at Okahu Bay, Auckland, on the day the *Hawaiki Nui* arrived in December 1985.

I met Matahi and told him of my plan to start waka ama paddling in the North and to start building canoes. Matahi encouraged me and told me he wanted to do the same thing in the Gisborne/East Cape area.

With the high unemployment in both areas, especially amongst the Maori people, we were able to take advantage of training schemes funded by the government to start these projects. The people of Pawarenga got behind the project wholeheartedly and made it happen.

By early 1987 we had a work-training scheme in place; building canoes and paddles and learning the art of paddling and handling them. Ocean knowledge, surf skills and swimming were very much a part of the program.

About the same time, I met a Samoan named Pili Muaulu who lived on the coast near Whangarei. He told me of his father's dream to find a suitable log to carve a traditional Samoan Pao Pao, a small two person fishing canoe. Coincidently I had a

Kris talks with his "Midgets". Development of waka ama at youth level is seen as paramount to the growth of waka ama sport in Aotearoa.

friend who had a suitable log on his property who I managed to talk into donating. As a result, our trainees, Pili and his family built the first traditional Samoan canoe in New Zealand.

The training scheme in Pawarenga eventually evolved into Nga Hoe Horo O Pawarenga (*the fast paddles of Pawarenga*)

and Matahi's group in Gisborne became Mare Kura Canoe Club. Pili's extended family formed a club called Mitamitaga Ole Pasefika Va'a Alo (*pride of the Pacific canoe club*) of Ngunguru. These three clubs along with one other in Okahu, Auckland, represented the original four clubs of New Zealand.

In May 1987 at the launching of our first canoe in Pawarenga, a meeting was held to form a national outrigger canoe association. The three founding members of the association named Tatou Hoe O Aotearoa (*all the paddlers of Aotearoa*), were Hga Hoe Horo O Pawarenga, Mitamitaga Ole Pasefika Va'a Alo of Ngunguru and Mare Kura of Gisborne. Immediately we started plans to bid for the 1990 IPCF World Outrigger Canoe Sprints.

In July 1987 a team of NZ paddlers, Matahi and myself travelled to Tahiti to participate in the Turai Festival races. On this trip we gained a lot of experience in paddling and racing Polynesian canoes.

In June 1988, Pili and myself attended the first international regatta held in Apia, Western Samoa. Whilst there, we spoke of our newly formed association and our wish

New Zealand National Championships 1995 – Junior ("Midget") crews.

to host the 1990 World Sprints. When we returned we formally adopted a constitution and elected officers for the association. Matahi was elected president, Pili as vice president and myself as executive committee.

In August of the same year, teams for Mare Kura and Nga Hoe Horo travelled to Hawaii to participate in the World Sprints at Keehi Lagoon, Honolulu, each with one men's and one women's crew. Whilst there we put in our bid for the 1990 titles and we won the honor.

Much had to be done including the building of a fleet of canoes which was left to me – sixteen six-person canoes. Although we were supposed to build the newly adopted IPCF hull we had problems in getting it and were instructed by Mary Jane Kahanamoku to "do the best we could with what we had".

The 1990 Canoe

We had begun waka ama with two Tahitian style canoes which were given to Matahi by Edward Mamaatua. The hull was altered to be as close to the IPCF canoe whilst keeping in mind New Zealand ocean conditions. New decks and ama were designed and a mould was made.

In re-designing and building the 1990 canoes the over-riding idea was to build for New Zealand conditions, so that the canoes would subsequently be useable for both offshore racing and flat water sprints.

These canoes became the nucleus fleet for outrigger canoe sport in Aotearoa. We built them to last and perform and they have. As of this writing they are still in service and still remain the most popular

Kris Kjedlson and Bo Herbert – Pawarenga, Hokianga, Northland 1989 with a prototype of the "1990 Canoe". In the background a traditional Waka Te Te (Fishing Canoe).

design in New Zealand.

The vast majority of W6 canoes in New Zealand are the 1990 design. Their one fault is that they are a little hard to turn. By putting a little more rocker in later models, the turning improved.

As a result of the sprints held in Orakei Basin in Auckland which were a resounding success, waka ama was finally up and really running. Since this time, outrigger canoe sport in NZ has enjoyed phenomenal growth. Today there are over thirty-three clubs and two regional associations; Taitokerau Polynesian Canoe Association in the far north and Auckland Region Outrigger Canoe Association which are members of our national organization recently re-named Nga Kaihoe O Aotearoa (*the paddlers of Aotearoa*).

Whilst most of the clubs have been located in the upper half of the North Island, in the last couple of years the sport has been spreading south with a lot of growth in the Wellington area and with two clubs starting up recently in the South Island.

In the last few years, NZ paddlers have had a number of international successes:

1992 At the fifth IPCF World Sprint Titles in Sacremento California, my son Maui Kjeldsen took gold in the Junior Men's solo. Corrina Gage took silver in the Open Women's solo and Tarawera Outrigger Canoe Club's Open Men won a silver in the 500m OC6 and Bronze in the 3000m.

1993 The NZ outrigger canoe team finished second in the Hamilton Island forty-two km marathon and fifth in the Bankoh Moloka'i Hoe in Hawaii out of seventy-five teams.

1994 At the sixth IPCF World Sprint Titles in Apia, Western Samoa, NZ paddlers won twenty-one medals, equal with that of Tahiti in medal count and jointly winning the championships.

Corrina Gage again taking a silver and Raipoia Brightwell (Matahi's wife) taking a bronze. Aaron Herbert of Nga Hoe Horo Canoe Club, Pawarenga won gold in the Junior Men 19 and Under solo and Spence and Gene Pospicil also of Nga Hoe Horo taking home the gold and bronze medals in the Junior Men 16 and Under solo event.

1994 New Zealand Nationals – Mitamitaga Ole Pasefica Waka Tauruа (Double Canoe) team.

Above: Mitamitaga Men – Sugar Loaf Race 1995
Below: Nga Hoe Horo Men – Sugar Loaf Race 1995

1995 A NZ women's selection was invited to travel to Tahiti to compete against the top Tahitian women's teams in the RFO Tahiti Marathon in April.

They finished first and in doing so inspired the Tahitians to put more energy into their women's programs having mostly concentrated on their men's teams.

In September Maui Kjeldsen and Aaron Herbert were invited to compete in the prestigious Super AITO long distance solo outrigger canoe race in Tahiti.

The Super AITO or Budweiser Channel Va'a is a race from the island of Moorea to Point Venice on Tahiti, a distance of thirty kilometres in solo outrigger canoes without rudders. The top twenty-five men finishers in a previously held AITO race of about twenty kilometres qualify to start in the Super AITO race along with invited paddlers

Mitamitaga Ole Pasefika Mens Team – Hauraki Hoe 1993

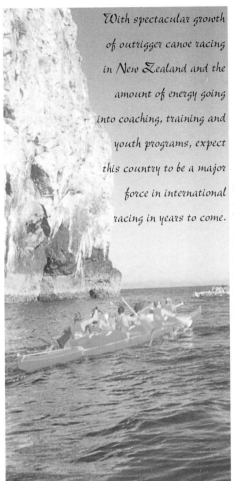

With spectacular growth of outrigger canoe racing in New Zealand and the amount of energy going into coaching, training and youth programs, expect this country to be a major force in international racing in years to come.

Canoe Surfing
AOTEAROA
Kris Kjeldsen

SURFING WHETHER ON BOARDS OR CANOES, IS NOT A NEW SPORT IN AOTEAROA. AS WAS THE CASE THROUGHOUT THE REST OF POLYNESIA. THE ABILITY TO NEGOTIATE BREAKING WAVES IN CANOES OR ON SURFBOARDS WAS A SURVIVAL SKILL. IT GAVE THE ANCIENT MAORI ACCESS TO OFFSHORE FISHING ALONG WAVE BATTERED COASTS AND A WAY TO RETURN SAFELY TO SHORE. THESE SURFING SKILLS WERE PRACTICED FOR PLEASURE AS WELL AS NECESSITY.

Canoe surfing contests were witnessed by early European visitors to the shores of Aotearoa. The steerer whose canoe and crew caught the most waves and got the longest and best rides gained both mana and respect.

A classic example of this was recorded by WH Skinner (1857-1946) who described how he had set up a meeting with a Taranaki chief, Te Rangi of Mokau. Skinner arrived at the village to find it deserted. Not what he had expected. He was directed to the beach where Te Rangi was competing in an annual canoe surfing competition.

When Skinner found them, Te Rangi and his crewman were heading out for another ride. Skinner described how the crowd cheered Te Rangi and his crewman and how no-one could out ride Te Rangi.

He sat statue-like, steering paddle firmly grasped as he concentrated intently

from overseas. Maui finished third.

Earlier in May, four men in two teams from New Zealand journeyed to Hawaii to compete in Walter Guild's Kaiwi Challenge a forty mile paddle from Moloka'i to Oahu in solo outrigger canoes.

In fairly normal Kaiwi Channel conditions of five to six foot swell out of the north and twenty to twenty-five knot northeast trades, Maui and his team mate, Paul Wilford finished eighth overall out of approximately fifty-three teams.

on the shape and movement of the wave. The most lasting impression of my mind in this surfing incident was that of the poise and skill of Te Rangi Tuataka Takere, the high born, as he sat statue-like . . . his fine muscular figure and clean cut tatooed features . . . a grand picture of pure Maoridom as it had been for centuries prior to AD 1884.

There are not many activities as exhilarating or exciting as flying along the face of a wave in an outrigger canoe. Today the sport of *waka-ama* surfing is undergoing a revival. Since this revival in 1987, a number of paddlers have travelled to Hawaii for races and have picked up the "stoke" and a few skills from their Hawaiian cousins and friends, today the undisputed masters of canoe surfing.

Back in New Zealand those paddlers find plenty of good canoe surf to put what they have learned into practice. Ideal conditions are found on river mouth and harbour bars with an incoming, near high tide when there is a good swell running.

The canoe surfing centres in Aotearoa are the Whangape Harbour Bar and Raglan on the west coast of the North Island, the Ngunguru River Bar, Ohope Beach and Gisborne on the east coast. Some memorable waves have also been surfed at Tokerau Beach, Muirwai Beach, Piha, Otaki Beach and the Whakatane Bar.

To date, most outrigger canoe surfing in Aotearoa has been in six person and single canoes, but recently four person canoes have been built specifically for surfing. They have lots of rocker and maneuverability similar to the surfing canoes used in Hawaii.

In these smaller vessels people are learning to turn, cut back and manoeuvre

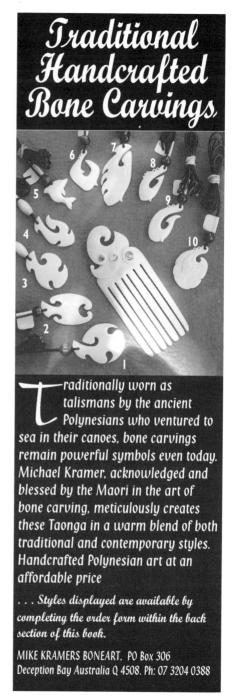

Solo outrigger canoe surfing Ngunguru River Mouth.

all over the face of the right type of wave. The best type of wave is a full, easy breaking swell from three to eight feet. People have learned to stay away from hard breaking, hollow, curling sets.

There have been a lot of thrills, spills, broken equipment and some minor injuries as part of the learning experience, but if reasonable care is taken, the right wave chosen and everyone in the crew can handle themselves in the event of a capsize, it can be a relatively safe way to get "big thrills". However, there are always those who will push things to the limits and take higher risks for greater thrills and sometimes greater spills.

As a general rule you should try to ride left breaking waves, angling away from the break on the left shoulder, with the ama up on the face of the wave. If you are surfing predominantly right-hand breaks, the ama should be rigged on the right side of the waka so it can be up on the wave face.

If you are trying to surf right breaking waves with the ama rigged on the left it is more than likely you will capsize, causing the canoe to go over the to of the ama. This can do damage to the canoe, kiato and paddlers. On the other hand if you are angling along a wave with the ama slightly up on the wave face and you flip, the ama goes over the waka with (usually) a minimum of trauma. The paddles are then quickly collected, the canoe righted, bailed out and you are paddling off to catch another wave much refreshed!

Waka Taua (War Canoes) Surfing Waitangi, Bay of Islands 1990

Canoe Surfing Ngunguru River Mouth

Maori canoe terms.

Models by Timber Treasures Australia.

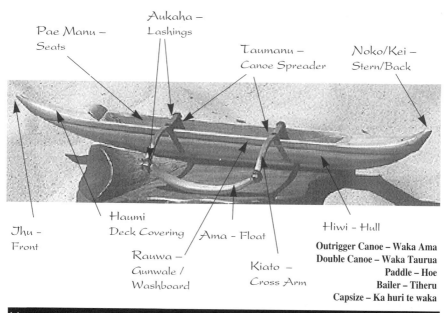

Aukaha – Lashings

Pae Manu – Seats

Taumanu – Canoe Spreader

Noko/Kei – Stern/Back

Ihu – Front

Haumi Deck Covering

Ama – Float

Rauwa – Gunwale / Washboard

Kiato – Cross Arm

Hiwi – Hull

Outrigger Canoe – Waka Ama
Double Canoe – Waka Taurua
Paddle – Hoe
Bailer – Tiheru
Capsize – Ka huri te waka

Hawaiian canoe terms.

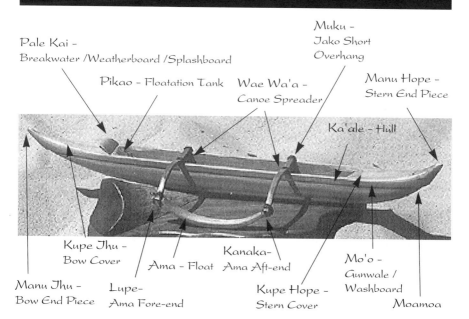

Pale Kai – Breakwater /Weatherboard /Splashboard

Pikao – Floatation Tank

Wae Wa'a – Canoe Spreader

Muku – Jako Short Overhang

Manu Hope – Stern End Piece

Ka'ale – Hull

Manu Ihu – Bow End Piece

Kupe Ihu – Bow Cover

Lupe – Ama Fore-end

Ama – Float

Kanaka – Ama Aft-end

Kupe Hope – Stern Cover

Mo'o – Gunwale / Washboard

Moamoa

− POSTCARD FROM GUAM −

In 1993 the Guam Kayak and Outrigger Federation (PROA) was formed in the knowledge that outrigger paddling was an important part of the history and culture of Guam through the original inhabitants, the Chamorro. In 1994 the MIcronesian Games held on Guam made outrigger canoe racing an official event with participants from Palau, Pohnpei, Marshalls and the Caroline island of Puluwat. From this the Marianas Paddlesports Racing Association (MPRA) was formed. Ka'nu Culture will be visiting Guam soon for a full story.

Sunset at Tumon Bay Guam. Photo Don Seery.

Paddling Fluid and Food

The value of good nutrition and the effect it has on paddling performance is now widely accepted. However, many paddlers live with the belief that it's good enough to simply improve their diet just prior to an event, when in truth it is the year-round diet that is most crucial to consistent paddling performance.

We are all familiar with the expression, "rubbish in, rubbish out". Well that pretty much describes the consequence of consuming food and drink of poor nutritional quality. It ultimately serves to stress the body and limit paddling potential.

If time is your enemy, then improved diet and fluid intake will definitely help you lift your performance without having to paddle that extra hour or run that extra mile. Whilst everyday demands can keep us off the water or away from the gym, the most obvious and inescapable reality is we still have to eat and drink. So why not do it right – get the extra edge without working up a sweat! Is this good stuff or what?

There has been in recent times, a huge growth in high energy, carbohydrate, snack bars and drinks containing minerals, salts (and all manner of voodoo) to fuel you up. They seem to come into their own where regular drinks and snacks won't deliver the same quick energy – where a quick fix is in order: in the case of marathon paddling of over an hour; or perhaps for those who haven't followed an adequate pre-race diet.

Extraordinary exertion demands extraordinary fuel intake. The more we push ourselves (at the mercy of sadistic race organizers competing to create the longest, the meanest and the mostest races) the more fuel and fluid is needed.

Outrigger distance paddling is on the

increase as far as participation numbers and also the number of events on offer around the Pacific. The nature of these races is essentially the very heart of what outrigger canoe racing is all about – endurance.

Not only is this happening in six person canoes but also in solo events which are now experiencing a massive surge of new participants who are looking for longer, harder races.

This is great to see, but it does demand that paddlers need to grasp the importance of quality and quantity of what is consumed daily. Then there's that other essential ingredient – fluid, prior to, during and after paddling, which takes on ever greater significance as race distances and air temperatures increase.

So you're ready to go. Fueled up and feeling like a coiled spring. Or ill-prepared, already partially dehydrated and running on empty – doomed from the start. Preparation through adequate fluid intake and food for fuel is essential for athletic demands. If outrigger canoe racing is a part of your lifestyle, then so should be an appropriate diet, in order for you to both train and race with the maximum amount of stored energy reserves, ensuring that you reach your full potential.

Australian nutritionist Di Barr, who works with many paddlers (outrigger canoeing and other disciplines) outlines guidelines for food and fluid intake, before, during and after exertion.

There you stand, paddle in hand, feeling taught and terrific. Ready to take on the ocean and all comers. Despite your hours of training – paddling, running, gym sessions – and an overall feeling of fitness and euphoria, without the right fuel, your performance will inevitably turn into a fizzer.

Daily training puts special demands on the body which in turn create unique nutritional needs. These must be met if you are to produce the best possible results in both training and competing.

Nutritional requirements of paddlers are based upon the general principles that everyone should follow for healthy eating. Except more of it, providing enough energy to allow you to train longer and harder – leading to an overall improvement in fitness, strength and performance.

Food and liquid consumption for the active paddler, falls into three categories: Everyday consumption – a high quality, high energy diet to sustain you daily. Fuelling up consumption – prior to an event, to ensure you have maximum energy stores for the effort required. Pre-event or last-minute consumption.

The most critical concept to grasp, is that it is your training diet which holds the greatest potential to affect your performance, together with the quality and content of your training.

As we are all unique in body size, energy needs, likes and dislikes, we need to create an individual dietary plan. It's important to work-in with those around you too, making your plan more achievable. (Jf you fly alone you can please yourself.) Appetite and body weight are good guides as to whether you are achieving a balance between energy expenditure and food intake.

Jf you are trying to lose body fat and gain muscle mass, the same guidelines still apply. You should not go hungry nor should you lose weight rapidly or unnecessarily. Weight loss in the weeks before an event can be dangerous.

Carbohydrates

Carbohydrates are the most important fuel source for exercising muscles. Their bi-product glycogen, is stored in the liver and muscle tissue to make up your energy reserves.

This is your energy store and needs to be continually refilled from carbo's in your diet. The more you exercise the greater your carbohydrate requirement will be.

Failure to refuel muscles after each training session will gradually deplete glycogen stores causing ineffective training and fatigue. Jt is important to recover carbo stores between sessions. There are two forms of carbohydrates:

Complex carbohydrates – cereals and grains (bread, rice, pasta), legumes (peas, beans, lentils), vegetables and fruit. These highly nutritious, high carbohydrate foods are also a source of vitamins, minerals and fibre. They represent the preferred sources of carbohydrate as they are absorbed and released gradually providing a more constant output of energy, thus ideal for prolonged exercise.

Simple carbohydrates – sugars in all their forms (honey, candies, soft drinks). Sugars can be used to top up your energy in the form of a quick "hit", breaking down quickly and being rapidly absorbed into the blood. They effectively "spike" blood sugar and insulin levels – which is why they affect some people drastically and adversely. Jntake should not exceed ten to fifteen percent of your daily total. Jf tolerated, they may be useful during or after exercise sessions.

For extra paddle power and pull, plan your meals and snacks around nutritious, complex carbohydrates. Aim to make up more than half (and as much as eighty percent) of your total food intake with these foods, depending on how heavily you train.

An ideal diet for training, competition and recovery must –

- **ensure an adequate intake of all nutrients; carbohydrates, proteins, fats, vitamins, minerals and fluids, to meet your requirements**
- **allow you to attain and sustain an appropriate level of body fat and body weight**
- **fit in with your lifestyle, juggling training, work and relationships.**

You will need to –

- **eat plenty of complex carbohydrates • eat less fats and oil • ensure adequate fluid intake • include calcium-rich foods • include iron-rich foods and • keep it simple!**

Fats and oils

Dietary fat provides essential fatty acids and fat soluble vitamins necessary to maintain health, but the typical diet contains far more fat than required.

Excess fat in the diet leads to excess fat in the blood, tissues and body. This not only decreases your power to weight ratio, but displaces some of your energy stores. Fat in the diet is either added –

• butter, margarine, oil, cream, sour cream, mayonnaise, salad dressing, tahini, nut butter, avocado.

or hidden –

• in dairy products, meats, fast foods, chocolates, bakery food.

Aim to make your diet low fat, but not no fat –

• cut back on oil in cooking
• eat lean meats, removing fat and skin before cooking
• eat low fat dairy products (fat reduced cheese)
• limit fast food and bakery food.

Proteins

Proteins are the basic building blocks of human tissue. All proteins are made up of amino acids some of which can be produced by the body, others we must get from food.

As you eat more food to meet increased energy requirements, you will usually be meeting your protein needs. remember an excess of protein in your diet will not build muscle tissue – it will be stored as body fat.

If you are wishing to bulk up, you should be looking at a diet high in complex carbohydrate, combined with a strength training program. Protein based muscle building powders are generally skim milk powder based. So if you think you need extra protein, add skim milk powder to your low fat milk – for a cheaper alternative!

Meat, poultry, seafood, eggs and low fat dairy products are excellent sources of protein. Some are also sources of iron, calcium and zinc and are complete proteins, containing all essential amino acids.

Iron and zinc strengthen the immune system and iron is essential for transporting oxygen in the blood to the muscles. Deficiency of this oxygen carrier can cause fatigue and poor performance, therefore adequate iron intake is essential. Taking Vitamin C at the same time as a meal high in iron will enhance your body's ability to absorb this essential mineral.

Legumes (peas, beans lentils) are a good source of protein and carbohydrate – low in fat but a poor source of iron. Vegetarians who eat legumes, nuts, eggs and dairy or soy products should have no problem meeting protein needs, however you may need to watch your iron intake.

For those who do not include eggs or dairy products in their diet, it is important to choose the right combinations of incomplete protein foods at each meal in order to ensure adequate supply of all amino acids.

Calcium maintains muscle tone and contraction and strength of bones. It's necessary to eat calcium containing foods daily. Sources of calcium include dairy products (choose low fat varieties) or for lactose intolerance, careful selection of leafy green vegetables, tinned fish, soy milk or possibly a calcium supplement.

Fluids

Be aware and beware that thirst is not a good indicator of when you need to replenish your system. By the time you feel thirsty, you are already dehydrated. Thirst is a delayed response to the need to take in fluid – the well is already dry! Performance is compromised by dehydration in several ways – fatigue, decreased anaerobic capacity, cramps, loss of concentration, gastric upset and even collapse.

Many factors combine to lead to exhaustion, nausea and dehydration. Dehydration is not always related to having consumed too little, but could be a factor of drinking fluid replacement or carbohydrate drinks mixed at too high a concentration. It is particularly crucial to experiment with the commercially made

fluid replacement drinks and high energy carbo snacks during training. Do not leave it until race day on the assumption that the magic elixir will give you all the energy you will need. Your body is a complex organism that responds to foods and stress in varying degrees of uniqueness.

Fluid loss is not only by sweat through the skin, but also via the breath. Strenuous exercise, leads to rapid, deeper breathing which increases fluid loss. Whilst conditioned paddlers may be able to tolerate up to eight percent of water loss relative to their body weight, after a two percent loss the central nervous system, the core temperature and pulse rate begin to be affected. Once the loss is three or four percent, performance can be reduced by as much as seven percent.

Get into the habit of drinking fluids before, during and after padding. Water is suitable for most training sessions under one hour, whilst commercial sports drinks and cordials will give you extra energy during longer sessions. During extremely hot weather water is best as it is easily absorbed. Sports drinks can hinder water absorption which is why generally they should be diluted.

High water content in the air (humidity) prevents rapid evaporation of sweat which is how we cool and prevent overheating. Subsequently paddling in high humidity with high air temperatures presents the greatest risk as our body temperature continues to rise and fluid loss is increased.

With excessive water loss by sweat we can be at risk of reduced blood pressure which in turn stresses the muscles by depleting them of oxygen. If left unchecked this ultimately interferes with the flow of blood from the body's inner core to the outer skin surface, which can lead to a shutting down of the sweating process in an attempt to conserve fluid, leading to a raised core temperature which is potentially life threatening. Be aware of how much sweat you are losing. If sweating ceases, you need to take action!

Hydration is paramount. Stay as well hydrated as possible in all conditions. In the cold your muscles are often working harder producing heat through motion and in staying warm. Hydrate even when it's cold.

To estimate sweat loss weigh yourself immediately before and after a session. Each kilogram of weight lost equals one litre of fluid lost or each pound equalling sixteen fluid ounces. Aim to keep the loss below 800g (one and three quarter pounds) in any one session, by taking enough fluids during training. Remember to account for hot weather. Replace the deficit fully after training.

Many paddlers start hydrating by drinking water twenty-four hours before an event until the urine is clear, then follow this with electrolyte and mineral replacements.

During short races or sprints it is impractical and unnecessary to drink. Make rehydration a top priority afterwards, especially if you have another race later.

For races of sixty to ninety minutes or more, water should be adequate. Sports drinks (diluted), defizzed soft drink and, diluted cordials are satisfactory. Go with what you prefer to taste and remember to practice during training.

Start fluid intake early in the event, with 150–250ml taken every quarter hour. Cool fluids are more refreshing. For events exceeding ninety minutes you will need to refuel your depleted glycogen stores as well, which are low to empty after about ninety minutes of continuous exercise. Do this by a carbo intake of 30-50g per hour –

- 500-800ml of diluted sports drink
- two 50g pure carbo Squeezies (if you're drinking water)
- jelly candy is popular with those able to tolerate the sugar hit.

Fueling up

Taper training five or six days before an event so you can fuel up on glycogen. One or two days before an event increase your intake of complex, low fat carbohydrate foods. You may need to eat reduced fibre to accommodate the increased intake.

If you are competing in an endurance event (ninety minutes or longer of continuous effort) you will have extreme carbohydrate-glycogen requirements. Fuelling up should be started three days before. Make greater use of simple carbohydrates. You may wish to use supplements such as carbo loading powders to ensure you avoid feeling bloated. Most important, make sure you bring adequate fluid for these events.

Once you have established an ideal diet, only minimal changes will need to be made in the days leading up to a race. Remember we are all different, so you will need to experiment with carbohydrates and general diets to see what works for you.

Pre-event fuelling up

Two to four hours before, eat a meal which is high in carbohydrate, low in fat and fibre – cereal and low fat milk; toast or muffin with honey, or banana; canned spaghetti; pancakes with syrup, fruit or low fat yogurt; or a low fat smoothie; or creamed rice with low fat milk and honey.

If you tend to be nervous and not able to eat, a liquid meal replacement may be more suitable. Take this one or two hours before the race to avoid problems.

An hour and a half prior to the race, top up your carbohydrate stores and fluids with fruit juice, cordial or diluted sports drinks. Try to get more or less half a litre. Practice this during training!

Thirty minutes before drink only water. Some people may be sensitive to blood glucose level changes caused by intake of sugars, especially in the hour before an event.

Guidelines for the race season –
- **one or two days before increase carbo's**
- **fuel up glycogen stores to combat fatigue**
- **eat an appropriate pre-race meal**
- **ensure adequate hydration – before, during and after the event**
- **ensure replacement of carbohydrates during longer events**
- **eat and drink to recover after the event**

Recovery

Start drinking fluids immediately after your training session or event. Water is usually the most accessible and practical rehydrator but sports drinks serve a purpose to replace carbohydrates and electrolytes. Replenish glycogen stores. Optimal uptake in the muscles is within the first two hours after exercise. It is best to have carbohydrates within fifteen to thirty minutes after strenuous exercise.

Consume one or two serves from the list below (providing 50g of carbohydrate) in the first hour and similar quantities every two hours until you can get back your normal eating pattern.

Commercially prepared replenishments –
• 800ml sports replenishment drink
• 500ml fruit juice, defizzed soft drink
• 250ml Lucozade, Gatorade
• jelly beans 50g.
Food based replenishments –
• low fat milk plus fruit as a smoothie
• fruit, three pieces
• yogurt (low fat) and fruit juice
• sandwich, honey, banana, jam
• cereal with low fat milk.

An integral part of strenuous exercise and nutritional recovery is to replace fluid and electrolyte loss (sports drinks); replenish glycogen stores (sports drinks, soft drinks, juices); and repair damage and prevent the symptoms of fatigue.

Alcohol is not a good rehydrator as it can interfere with the refuelling and rehydrating process and also delays tissue repair. If you are bruised or have strained muscles you should refrain from alcohol for twenty four hours.

As a paddler you need to be in touch with the demands you are making of your body and take steps to ensure it receives correct and adequate fuel daily. You need to pay special attention to fluid replacement as dehydration during strenuous exercise is positively dangerous.

₼ydration Systems

luid replenishment is absolutely crucial in maintaining your physiological capability to perform at your best. A personal hydration system is necessary for training or racing any longer than thirty minutes. In the case of distance events where no change-overs are permitted, you must have an adequate supply of fluids with you, attached either to the canoe or to yourself. The fact is, a quality hydration system should be seen as the next immediate purchase after that other essential tool, the paddle. It is a vital piece of equipment which every sensible-minded paddler should own as standard equipment.

Commercial hydration systems have over the last ten years gained greater market place acceptance in catering for the rapid growth of outdoor pursuits of every kind – which seem to be ever evolving into more extreme and radical hybrids, almost on a daily basis.

Hydration systems have long been accepted in paddle-sport disciplines such as kayaking and marathon canoeing, but have been slow to find popular usage amongst outrigger canoe paddlers. This it seems is due in part to lack of knowledge about the need for such devices and the fact that

many of the available systems are non-specific to outrigger canoeing.

A variety of commercially produced hydrating systems provide for hands-free operation, but often require you to make a support for the tubing to allow you to drink whilst paddling. Even then you will often need to momentarily pause to guide the tube to your mouth.

Attempts to rig up a system which puts the mouthpiece so close to your mouth you can reach it without having to guide it momentarily with your hand, are never particularly successful. The mouthpiece has

Staying hydrated is absolutely crucial to paddling performance and overall wellbeing.

to be so close, that it tends to repeatedly hit you in the face or move so as no matter how hard you try you cannot reach it.

Systems generally favour a sealed plastic bladder secured within an insulated fabric pouch which is strapped to the wearer or to equipment and the fluid transferred from bladder to mouth via a tube. Generally the user has to suck the fluid up, however some innovative designs work on a feed system based on pressure.

The Aquastream or Bikestream models work in this manner, whereby the fluid was pumped into a bladder under pressure. The action of biting down on a one-way valve at the mouthpiece causes fluid to be ejected into the mouth. It is a very efficient system, squirting a thin jet of water under pressure – so that the unaware might think they were experiencing a tonsillectomy. However, these are no longer available.

A problem experienced with this system, is that the valve sometimes remains open, so that long after you relinquish your bite, the fluid continues to squirt, leading to a severe rise in blood pressure! Occasionally the bladder would split due to its high pressure.

Most commercial models work on the suck-it-up-as-you-need-it technique via a one-way valve. Sucking can be tough when you don't have any suck left, but this is generally the most reliable option.

It is important to consider the following when choosing a hydration system –
•COMFORT WITH NO CHAFFING •FREEDOM OF MOVEMENT PADDLING OR SWIMMING •SEALED AGAINST SALT WATER IMMERSION •DURABILITY AND RESISTANCE TO SALT WATER •FULLY AND EASILY ADJUSTABLE •QUICK RELEASE •RELIABILITY IN FLUID DELIVERY •ADEQUATE VOLUME OF FLUID FOR YOUR NEEDS •LIGHT WEIGHT •AVAILABILITY OF SPARE BLADDERS, VALVES ETC.

Check out the stitching of the pouch and the quality of the insulation, if insulated. Importantly check out the bladder, the tubing and the mouthpiece. I have heard many paddlers say that some bladders are not always as tough as they should be, so make a careful study of the way it is moulded and sealed, also check the seal of the filler cap.

Consider how it might affect your paddling and swimming. Do you like to paddle without a shirt? Would the straps be annoying and distracting. What are your specific needs – are you a steerer, paddler or solo outrigger canoeist or all three?

Steerers are generally happy with back worn systems which generally carry larger volumes of fluid than hip or waist models – some up to three litres. Steerers who paddle iron or without change-over in distance races, may be in the canoe for as long as six hours, which means that without too much exaggeration, will need five or six litres of fluid, based on the litre per hour theory.

This would mean if wearing a two litre hydration system, you would require two spare bladders which would have to be easily changed during the race. However many steerers make do with the initial litre, then rely on water bottles passed to them from support boats.

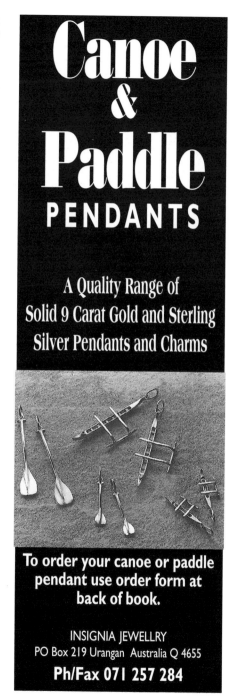

In the case of making change-overs it is impractical to have a hydration system attached to you or even to the canoe, so adequate pre-race hydration is crucial as is fluid intake when back on the support boat.

The favoured style in the case of a body worn system for paddlers (as opposed to steerers) is hip or waist worn. This presents less of a hindrance to upper body movement possessing less potential for chaffing under the arms or over the shoulders. For many women, this method of attachment has obvious merits.

Attaching systems to canoes is often done by setting up a crude receptacle into which a plastic bottle of some nature is placed and a tube run from it to the paddler,

The simple effort of taking a regular plastic soda bottle, attaching a bent wire coathanger with some tape and hanging it over the gunwale is a step in the right direction to organising your personal hydration needs.

or simply pulled out and fluid taken straight from the bottle. Unavoidably it may be necessary to use glue, rivets, or a bent coathanger over the gunwale or cover loops or vast amounts of duct tape to affix your bottle holder to the canoe. Keep in mind that not all clubs are too happy with permanent defacing of canoes. Something for canoe manufacturers to consider might be the addition of an adjustable bottle holder for each seat.

Beware that an inherent danger of attaching a water container or bladder to the gunwale, seat or cover loops and the tubing to yourself, is that should you huli (capsize) you could get tangled up. You want a quick release method worked out and you will need to practice it. A tube which is easily accessible and put to your mouth quickly then replaced is safer and less of a hindrance and means you will only miss one or two strokes each drink.

Stowage of bottles in canoes is a serious matter and often poorly managed. Whilst a bottle with a tube is often easily arranged, last minute efforts to attach bottles can see them simply being thrown into the bottom of the canoe. If more than one paddler uses this method, identification of your particular bottle can become a challenge, to say nothing about the sound of containers rolling around and stubbing your toes on them as you switch.

Bike Bottle attached to solo canoe.

Solo outrigger canoe paddlers can be very creative in attaching bottle holders to their personal canoes. One of the most simple and favoured methods is the attachment of a bike bottle set up to the canoe close to the foot wells. This can then either have a tube running from it or can simply be pulled out.

Taking fluids whilst in the canoe comes down to two real choices. You can opt for a commercial suck-it-up-as-you-need-it system for biggish bucks or a make your own for less or virtually no bucks. Whichever you choose, you must practice with your hydrating system so that you are comfortable with it and satisfied with the amount of fluid it provides.

Systems which hold little more than a litre, will last as long as an hour and a half provided you have taken the precaution to hydrate twenty-four hours beforehand . The amount of fluid which your system contains is crucial. You may need more than one system or perhaps a replacement bladder.

One last option and by far the cheapest is not to have a water container at all. Some of us are just so damn tough we don't need fluids, right? Wrong. The bottom-line is, whether training or racing, hydration is crucial – so get organised.

Now, let's get back to the more serious considerations of choosing a commercial system. One thing is for sure most have been developed around the needs of cyclists, dirtbike riders and hikers, whose upper bodies are relatively static when compared with paddlers.

Because of a paddler's upper body movements there are some problems associated with strap-ons as mentioned earlier where straps run over the shoulders and under the arms. Any fear of chafing can

And when it's all over, you can hydrate in another way. Nothing like a hose down after paddling hard in high humidity and air temperatures.

however be generally alleviated by wearing a wet-shirt or t-shirt or by the addition of foam padding. A steerer's movements are less repetitive and therefore a back worn system is perhaps of no real hindrance.

Consider also that this design adds weight to the upper torso which requires a degree of extra effort. When all six paddlers are wearing back pack style hydration systems the centre of gravity on each paddler is effectively raised, marginally de-stabilizing the canoe. Additional weight at the waist or lower is definitely preferable. Worn at the waist, a system does not have the same degree of effect on the upper body and is therefore more comfortable.

Hydration Systems from the Ka'nu Shop

Outrigger canoeists require a hydration system as part of their personal equipment. It is all part of taking a responsible, professional approach to one's sporting commitment to be the best you can. The Ka'nu Shop can now recommend and supply a range of three different hydration systems.

- The Camelbak®- worn on the back,
- The Go-Be® – worn on the waist • The Ride'R™ – worn by the canoe!

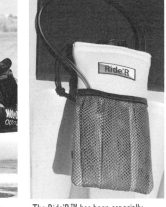

The Camelbak®. Available in a range of volumes; 32, 50 and 70 (2lt) ounces. Fully insulated back worn hydration systems. 70 ounce system weighs only 8 ounces dry. SuperFlo Freedom Valve™ – split bite system; bite down and fluid is available, seals when bite is released. Quick release fully adjustable buckles. Non-chafe straps. Easy to refill and clean. Colours: Black, Bone and Azure Blue. Recommended for steerers. **$99.45**

The Hip Way to Stay Cool! The Go-Be® is a "Body Hugging Hydration System" worn around the hips. Fully insulated, uses the same split bite valve as the Camelback®. Zip pockets all around, super durable Cordura, breathable Apex® wicking mesh that's non chafing. Super comfortable, 50 ounce (1½lt) capacity. 14 ounce dry weight. Colour: Sagebrush, Eggplant, Black combo. Recommended for paddlers and solo canoeists. **$135.00**

The Ride'R™ has been especially designed for personal watercraft. Made using the finest materials, the Ride'R™ attaches to the side of the canoe with exclusive power suction cups anchored through a bungie matrix. 32 ounce (1lt) capacity, the Ride'R™ is perfect for solo outrigger canoes, surf-skis and other paddle craft where a smooth surface is available. **$108.00**

Order Form at back of book. All enquiries to the Ka'nu Shop at Batini Books
12 month guarantee with all Hydration Systems. Hydrate or Die®

Camelbak® Hydration System
Fastrak Systems, Inc. Texas USA.

Touted as the most efficient hydration system on the planet, the Camelbak® is everything it's cracked up to be, which is a relief in a world full of dodgy products and wanna-be's!

The first thing that strikes you about the Fastrak range of hydration systems, is the quality and attention to detail that has gone into their manufacture and design.

The Camelbak® Hydration System takes its name from the hump-like shape it forms when worn on the back. The no slosh, hands free drinking system is made in two sizes, a half Bak 32oz (1lt) volume and a 70oz (2lt) volume. Fluid is delivered through a tube via an innovative split bite valve.

Two models are available. The Thermobak is fully insulated keeping fluids hot or cold for up to four hours and the Icebak which is designed to conduct the temperature of the liquid in the reservoir to the user, by having a thinner insulating layer against the skin. When paddling in hot conditions you can fill the reservoir with near freezing fluid which has the net effect of lowering the core body temperature during paddling. Research has shown that this in turn reduces heart rates by as much as 6.5% whilst maintaining the same workrate. It can also dramatically reduce sweat loss by maintaining a lower core body temperature.

The split valve mouthpiece ensures that

Simple strapping arrangement with straps designed to minimize chafing. Bent wire can serve to hold the mouthpiece close to you. However a clip is available to attach the tube to your top clothing.

the system remains sealed in the event of being immersed in salt water. By biting on the tip of the valve a fine slit opens on the mouthpiece allowing fluid to pass through. On release it closes tight over.

Everything about the Camelbak® is to the highest standards both in terms of materials used and quality of manufacture.

Despite being a back worn system, the Camelbak® is still remarkably comfortable to wear. Paddling is not hindered, and chafing doesn't seem to be a problem. However it does comes down to the paddler's level of tolerance as you are always aware of wearing something back there and this fact alone may annoy some. For steerers paddling iron in changeover races the large 70oz volume makes good sense.

The Go-Be® Hydration System
Fastrak Systems, Inc. Texas USA

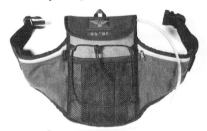

Again from Fastrak Systems, Inc. the Go-Be® is a waist or hip worn system which is very much more than just a hydration system, as with its zippered side pockets and rear mesh pocket now you can take along car keys, sun cream, money, gloves etc. Referred to as a "body hugging" hydration system the Go-Be® is as you would expect, fantastically constructed and designed.

The fully insulated system holds up to fifty ounces (1 1/2 lts) of hot or cold fluid for hours.

Its biggest advantage is the fact that it is worn on the waist or hips which allows the paddlers upper torso to be free of any restrictions. After testing the Go-Be® we felt it offered the paddler the best solution to their hydration needs in terms of comfort and the little extras that it provides. Of course it's not cheap, but then again nothing of high quality and durability is, but it's good value when you take into account that it doubles as both a decent sized bum-bag and hydration system in one.

Heavy duty in construction, the Go-Be® has a dry weight of 14oz and is adjustable for waist sizes from 26" (66cm) to 46" (116.8cm).

Worn on waist or hips, the Go-Be® is definitely a "Hip way to Hydrate".

The Bushy Bag System
Westcraft Canoeing Products. Australia.

The Westcraft Bushy Bag is as the manufacturers claim designed specifically for canoeing.

An insulated bag keeps fluid warm or cold though we suspect not to the same degree as the Camelbak® as it is of thinner gauge. The tubing is run from the inside of the pouch out of the bottom which differs from most systems and is then guided to the mouth passed through a series of web loops. In this respect the designers have catered to the needs of canoeists who need the mouthpiece readily available to them.

A simple sliding on/off valve permits the

A closer look at the Bushy Bag system's strapping arrangement.

user to allow water to pass or have it sealed. Having it sealed when not in use is preferable in case you end up in the water.

The reasonably wide diameter of the tubing delivers quite a large volume of water in one go and carrying capacity is certainly large enough, holding up to three litres.

The strapping arrangement is a little messy and perhaps the webbing is a little light weight. The strapping arrangement may also present problems for some ladies of larger chest size.

The system is probably more suited to steerers than to paddlers and its large capacity makes it good value for iron races.

CONCLUSION

Due to the fact that the outrigger canoe is an *open* canoe and that solo outriggers are *sit on top,* outrigger canoe paddlers can comfortably wear waist or hip hydration systems which not all kayak designs permit due to the enclosed nature of the seating position.

Even when wearing covers, the waist or hip worn system presents no problems and if anything it protects the body's mid region from cover burns.

The Bushy Bag and the Camelbak® are clearly well suited to kayak paddling where a waist or hip worn system may interfere with the canoe itself.

Back worn systems are also ideal for steerers who may wish to carry larger volumes of water when paddling iron. In terms of quality, attention to detail, function and durability the Camelbak® is undoubtedly a superior device. The Busy Bag is nonetheless efficient and offers a cheaper, functional alternative.

Beyond this the Go-Be® is the ant's pants for the paddler who wants a brilliant two in one hydration system and bum-bag – carrying not only your fluid but all those little extras for both on and off the ocean, whilst permitting freedom of movement so that you don't even know you're wearing it. The system makes an ideal partner in paddling and being of such high quality it will undoubtedly last for many seasons which in the long run, represents great value.

Canoe Attached Systems

The Ride'R™
FasTrak Systems, Inc. Texas USA.

FasTrak Systems, Inc. true to fashion with their eternal quest to keep the world's active people hydrated have a brilliant system which will overcome all the aggravation you've ever had in attaching a hydration system to your canoe or surfski – by means of giant suckers.

The Ride'R™ has two large suction cups which allow it to be attached to the canoe without the need to drill holes or use duct tape. Like any suction cap it requires a smooth surface.

The suckers work best on smooth gelcoat surfaces and attach well to solo canoes but generally have problems on textured surfaces such as the inside of a six-person canoe. To overcome this a smooth perspex plate could first be affixed to the inside of the canoe.

This hydration system was purpose designed for aquatic use, *whether cruising down the river or lake in a kayak/canoe; blasting with a personal water craft . . .*

Capable of carrying 32oz (1lt) of fluid the Ride'R™ is insulated and has the bite activated FreedomValve™ as featured on the Go-Be® and Camelbak® systems. The inclusion of a roomy mesh pocket allows you to take gloves, sun cream, power bars and the like with you, always a plus.

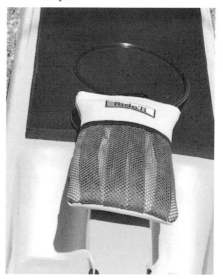

The giant suckers have great flexibility in terms of where they can be stuck not being attached directly to the pouch, but to an elasticated matrix. For ease of removal a release tab, pops the sucker away.

This is possibly the only system of its type and judging by the worldwide patent which warns *Don't even think about it*, the system will probably remain unique for some time.

If wearing a hydration system doesn't appeal, the Ride'R™ is the best alternative available. The tube, when not being used can be tucked into the meshing and removed when required, which seems the best method, in the case of canoe mounted systems.

Provided a good grip is achieved, in the event of capsize the system remains fast and does not break free like bottles in holders, which we all know, fall out and float away or end up rolling up and down the canoe.

Here the Rider'R™ has been attached between the footwells on a solo canoe. Naturally it works just as well on many other paddle craft including surf-skis. A mesh pocket is handy for bits and bobs. Below shows the mother suckers that do their job!

Brief Encounters

eing involved with outrigger canoe racing on an international level, makes it necessary to travel across the vast expanse of the Pacific Ocean, from one edge of the Pacific Rim to the other.

Talk to most any islander from Hawaii to Fiji, Tahiti to New Caledonia, New Zealand to Samoa, and you will find that the subject of outrigger canoeing and the canoe as a central artifact, will bring you to common ground.

Travel with an outrigger paddle in your hand throughout Oceania, and it seems you are carrying a universal symbol – an icon representative of a wide range of cultural groups of the region.

Standing in an airport in Fiji or Tahiti, casually holding your paddle as if it were a natural extension of yourself, you will naturally draw attention.

It seems the mere presence of the paddle transcends social or cultural barriers, stirs imaginations, igniting an inherent affinity between those who recognize its significance.

Here then is one such encounter, but I didn't have to go anywhere to experience it, for it happened on the telephone in the comfort of my own home . . . a canoeing bond, a cultural exchange.

I was having difficulty getting through to an overseas bookseller when an international directory assistant interrupted. I explained my problem and it wasn't long before we were in conversation about Ka'nu Culture.

Recognizing she had an accent I asked where she was from and it turned out it was Fiji. She was fascinated about the book and that I should have such a strong interest in canoes and was thrilled to have found someone who could converse in the language of the canoe.

She told me her grandfather was a canoe builder from Kabara Island in the Fijian Lau Group of islands and recounted a canoe story he used to tell about when they ventured into the forest to select a canoe tree, no one was allowed to talk. Not even to whisper. For if the tree was to hear, it would warp and twist itself so as to be no good for canoe building.

Her people believed they had come from Africa via India and that the canoe had been intrinsic to their migration.

This brief encounter confirmed to me once again that the canoe, its creation and symbolic representation is (apart from language itself) the central binding element of Melanesian, Micronesian and Polynesian cultures.

Transcending the intervention of missionaries and European invasion, the spirit of the canoe lives on.

International Race Results

Solo Open Women 500m Sprint
1	2.50.51	Kellie Edmunds	Brisbane
2	2.54.98	Therese Powell	Sydney
3	2.55.59	Simone Golik	Brisbane

Solo Master Women 500m Sprint
1	3.10.79	Jenny Hill	Noosa
2	3.11.84	Frances Grabbe	Mooloolaba
3	3.12.28	Joanne Fergusson	Capricorn

Solo Open Women 8km Marathon
1	1.08.38	Therese Powell	Sydney
2	1.14.03	Tanya Coert	Mooloolaba
3	1.17.39	Karin Maloney	Capricorn

Solo Master Women 8 km Marathon
1	1.12.09	Annie Harding	Sydney
2	1.14.03	Sam Aldwell	Mooloolaba
3	1.17.19	Nerada Tree	Noosa Heads

Open Women 16.1km Marathon
1	1.29.59		Panamuna 1
2	1.31.37		Sydney
3	1.32.29		Brisbane

Master Women 16.1km Marathon
1	1.37.53		Mooloolaba
2	1.38.53		Noosa Heads
3	1.39.08		Surfers Paradise

Open Women 2,000m Sprints
1	10.47.28		Sydney
2	10.54.11		Brisbane
3	11.05.41		Hawaii OCC

Master Women 2,000m Sprints
1	11.15.65		Surfers Paradise
2	11.17.60		Mooloolaba
3	11.28.90		Noosa Heads

Open Women 42.2km Marathon
1	4.22.53		Panamuna
2	4.26.50		Sydney
3	4.27.49		Hamilton Island

Master Women 42.2km Marathon
1	4.45.55		Capricorn Coast
2	4.47.08		Brisbane
3	4.59.57		Surfers Paradise

Solo Open Men 500m Sprint
1	2.20.68	John Foti	HCKT
2	2.25.64	Wyatt Jones	Hawaii OCC
3	2.31.22	J Somerville-Kimlin	Mooloolaba

Solo Master Men 500 m Sprint
1	2.23.23	Steve Cole	T Hawaii Mstrs
2	2.25.64	Walter Guild	
3	2.31.22	Todd Bradley	

Solo Open Men 9.6km Marathon
1	1.00.49	Jim Foti	HCKT
2	1.01.55	John Foti	HCKT
3	1.02.44	J Somerville-Kimlin	Mooloolaba

Solo Master Men 9.6km Marathon
1	1.02.36	Steve Cole	T Hawaii Mstrs
2	1.04.48	Mick Smith	Whitsunday
3	1.14.02	Bryan Davis	Whitsunday

Master Men 16.1km Marathon
1	1.16.51		Mooloolaba
2	1.17.42		Northcliffe Gold
3	1.18.53		Team Hawaii Mstrs

Open Men 2,000 Sprints
1	9.21.22		HCKT
2	9.25.00		Outrigger Australia
3	9.29.50		Outrigger Australia

Master Men 2,000 Sprints
1	9.54.89		Northcliffe Gold
2	10.03.38		Mooloolaba
3	10.04.78		Team Hawaii Mstrs

Open Men 42.2km Marathon
1	3.33.53		Outrigger Australia
2	3.37.08		Panamuna
3	3.40.55		HCKT

Master Men 42.2km Marathon
1	3.45.31		Mooloolaba
2	3.50.08		Team Hawaii Mstrs
3	3.51.17		Imua California

Fifteen associations from around the world were represented at the Fifth World Sprints in Apia and included American Samoa, Australia, Canada, Cook Islands (Raratonga), Fiji, Guam, Hawaii, Kalifornia, New Caledonia, New Zealand (Aotearoa), Northern California, Stahlo (USA), Tahiti, Wallis-Futuna and Western Samoa.

Junior Women Solo (16) 500m
1	3.17.95	Teraivetea Taruoura	Tahiti
2	3.28.90	Katherine Bumatay	Hawaii
3	3.34.62	Teipotemarama T Nikoia	Raratonga
4	3.49.34	Hokuala Johnson	HCRA
5	4.03.00	Lucinda Paoafaaite	Tahiti
6	4.08.52	Rahera Tiatia	Tahiti

Junior Women Solo (19) 500m
1	3.09.46	Lolita Firuu	New Caledonia
2	3.10.11	Hinatea Poroi	Tahiti
3	3.13.00	Maeva Temauri	New Caledonia
4	3.18.67	Moea Maono	New Caledonia
5	3.23.29	Kerri Cummins	Hawaii
6	3.37.53	Myriam Hmeun	New Caledonia

Master Women Solo (35) 500m
1	3.00.10	Heather Taylor	Canada
2	3.03.18	Sylie Auger	Tahiti
3	3.05.28	Ngarama Ngata	Aotearoa
4	3.09.01	Kim MacMillan	Canada
5	3.10.93	Brenda Flan	Canada
6	3.17.78	Judy Shandller	Canada

Open Women Solo 500 m
1	2.53.09	Jacqueline Webber	Canada
2	2.54.67	Corrina Gage	Aotearoa
3	2.58.08	Raipoia Brightwell	Aotearoa
4	3.02.72	Heather Taylor	Canada
5	3.05.55	Mena Tautu	Tahiti
6	3.08.01	Lolita Firuu	New Caledonia

Junior Women Six-person (16) 500m
1	2.47.23		Hawaii	HCRA
2	2.51.04	Vaai Lau Foe Kalapu A P	Western Samoa
3	3.00.92		Marina del Ray	Kalifornia

Junior Women Six-person (19) 500m

1	2.36.78	Nga Taiwhakaronga	Aotearoa
2	2.37.48	Hawaii	HCRA
3	2.38.08	Atafa Canoe Club	Western Samoa
4	2.38.50	New Caledonia National	New Caledonia
5	2.48.62	Mitamitanga	Aotearoa

Master Women (35) Six-person 500m

1	2.32.22	Hawaii	HCRA
2	2.33.73	Marei Kura	Aotearoa
3	2.34.51	Canada	CORA
4	2.34.76	Hui O Hawaii	N California
5	2.35.12	Canada	CORA
6	2.36.76	Malihini	Australia

Open Women Six-person 500m

1	2.21.71	Hawaii	HCRA
2	2.22.31	Ruahatu	Tahiti
3	2.23.19	Hawaii	HCRA
4	2.25.93	Te Waiariki Purea	Aotearoa
5	2.27.17	Rautere	Tahiti
6	2.29.38	Surfers Paradise	Australia

Junior Women Six-person 1000m

1	5.27.96	Nga Taiwhakarongo	Aotearoa
2	5.31.26	New Cal National	New Caledonia
3	5.35.67	Atafa Canoe Club	Western Samoa
4	5.37.89	Hawaii	HCRA
5	5.40.85	Haapu Huahine	Tahiti
6	5.48.11	Vaai Lau Foe Kalapu A P	Western Samoa

Master Women (35) Six-person 1000m

1	5.12.15	Canada	CORA
2	5.17.87	Hawaii	HCRA
3	5.20.43	Hui O Hawaii	N California
4	5.26.57	Mitamitanga	Aotearoa
5	5.29.63	Malihini	Australia

Open Women Six-person 2000

1	10.21.89	Hawaii	HCRA
2	10.28.79	Tu Waiariki Purea	Aotearoa
3	10.39.40	Ruahatu	Tahiti
4	11.07.03	Lami	Fiji
5	11.09.79	Kai Elua	Kalifornia
6	11.21.77	Leeward Kai	Hawaii

Junior Women (19) Twelve-person 500m

1	2.28.79	Nga Taiwhakarongo	Aotearoa
2	2.31.67	Haapu Huahine	Tahiti
3	2.33.37	Hawaii	HCRA
4	2.47.09	California	Kalifornia

Master Women (35) Twelve-person 500m

1	2.19.65	Canada	CORA
2	2.21.60	Kaitaia Dolphins	Aotearoa
3	2.22.33	Hawaii	HCRA
4	2.27.26	Hui O Hawaii	N California
5	2.28.03	Kai Elua	Kalifornia
6	2.36.21	Malolo	American Samoa

Open Women Twelve-person 500m

1	2.10.07	Hawaii	HCRA
2	2.12.02	Tahiti	Tahiti
3	2.17.75	Malihini	Australia
4	2.18.44	Canada	CORA
5	2.18.76	Te Waiariki Purea	Aotearoa
6	2.20.52	Kai Klua	Kalifornia

Junior Men Solo (16) 500m

1	2.49.87	Spence Pospisil	Aotearoa
2	2.50.21	Mark Tahuhuterani	New Caledonia
3	2.50.69	Gene Pospisil	Aotearoa
4	2.54.65	Julien Tavaearii	Tahiti

Junior Men Solo (19) 500m

1	2.38.04	Aaron Herbert	Aotearoa
2	2.40.10	Peter Simon Williams	Aotearo
3	2.40.33	Dale J Jefferson	Stahlo USA
4	2.41.24	Albert Teraiamano	Tahiti
5	2.45.82	Billy Tupea	Tahiti
6	2.46.60	Jim Farnum	Hawaii

Master Men Solo (40) 500m

1	2.37.14	Ieremia Temauri	New Caledonia
2	2.38.70	Mana Temaiana	Tahiti
3	2.39.11	Henri Vairaaroa	Tahiti
4	2.39.50	Alain Tuahine	Tahiti
5	2.44.42	Michel Arutahi	Tahiti
6	2.47.94	Nappy Napoleon	Hawaii

Open Men Solo 500 m

1	2.24.44	Karyl Maoni	Tahiti
2	2.26.19	Daniel Nuupure	Tahiti
3	2.27.18	Laughlin Lewis	Tahiti
4	2.28.57	Maui Kjeldsen	Aotearoa
5	2.31.33	John Foti	Hawaii
6	2.36.13	Armand Tauotaha	Tahiti

Junior Men Six-person (16) 500m

1	2.18.83	Nga Hoe Horo	Aotearoa
2	2.21.24	Atafa Canoe Club	Western Samoa
3	2.22.02	Mulivai Otara	Aotearoa
4	2.26.82	Hawaii	HCRA
5	2.47.35	Marina del Ray	Kalifornia

Junior Men Six-person (19) 500m

1	2.06.20	Mulivai Otara	Aotearoa
2	2.08.32	Vaai Lau Foe Kalapu A P	Western Samoa
3	2.08.64	Faaa	Tahiti
4	2.09.08	Atafa	Western Samoa
5	2.10.00	Faaroa Raiatea	Tahiti
6	2.12.02	Tarawera	Aotearoa

Master Men (40) Six-person 500m

1	2.04.49	Tahiti	Tahiti
2	2.04.87	Hawaii	HCRA
3	2.07.49	New Caledonia National	New Caledonia
4	2.07.70	Marei Kura	Aotearoa
5	2.14.66	Tai Tokerau	Aotearoa
6	2.17.26	Kai Elua	Kalifornia

Open Men Six-person 500m

1	1.54.02	Faaa	Tahiti
2	1.55.94	Hawaii 2	HCRA
3	1.58.02	Faaa	Tahiti
4	2.01.39	Waikiki Surf	Hawaii
5	2.05.94	Waikiki Surf	Hawaii
6	2.06.94	Hawaiki Nui	Aotearoa

Junior Men (19) Six-person 1000m

1	4.33.23	Mulivai Otara	Aotearoa
2	4.35.41	Atafa Canoe Club	Western Samoa
3	4.36.88	Faaroa Raiatea	Tahiti
4	4.37.51	Hawaii	HCRA
5	4.37.93	Tarawera	Aotearoa
6	4.39.98	Faaa	Tahiti

Master Men (40) Six-person 1000m

1	4.24.56	Tahiti	FTDV
2	4.26.28	Hawaii	HCRA
3	4.34.25	Marei Kura	Aotearoa
4	4.35.33	New Caledonia National	New Caledonia
5	4.48.83	Tai Tokerau	Aotearoa
6	4.52.49	Kai Elua	Kalifornia

Open Men Six-person 2000m

1	8.39.59	Faaa	Tahiti
2	8.49.27	Hawaii	HCRA
3	9.00.70	Waikiki Surf Club	Hawaii
4	9.10.69	Faaa	Tahiti
5	9.15.62	Hawaii	HCRA
6	9.18.37	New Caledonia National	New Caledonia

Junior Men (19) Twelve-person 500m

1	1.58.25	Tahiti	FTDV
2	1.58.52	Tarawera	Aotearoa
3	1.59.32	Nga Hoe Horo	Aotearoa
4	1.59.32	Atafa	Western Samoa
5	2.02.11	Hawaii	HCRA
6	2.03.05	Mulivai	Aotearao
7	2.22.74	Marina del Ray	Kalifornia

Master Men (40) Twelve-person 500m

1	1.58.05	Hawaii	HCRA
2	2.00.24	Marei Kura	Aotearoa
3	2.01.29	Kai Elua	KOA
4	2.01.76	Tahiti	FTDV

Open Men Twelve-person 500m

1	1.47.15	Tahiti	FTDV
2	1.51.08	Hawaii	HCRA
3	1.53.36	Waikiki Surf Club	Hawaii
4	1.54.00	Kai Elua	Kalifornia
5	1.54.37	Hawaiki Nui	Aotearoa
6	2.02.66	New Caledonia	New Caledonia

Queen Lili'uokalani Kona Coast, September 1995

15-18 Single Hull Female

1	2.09.28	Hawaiian Canoe & Kayak 1
2	2.18.21	Lokahi 1
3	2.21.04	Na Keiki O Ka Moi 5
4	2.29.48	Kawaihae 3

Iron Masters Female

1	2.16.25	Keauhou 7
2	2.17.27	Keauhou 8
3	2.21.17	False Creek 2
4	2.22.30	False Creek 3
5	2.24.23	Nakai E Walu 5
6	2.33.05	Nakai E Walu 6
7	2.33.15	Waikiki Yacht 5
8	2.40.57	Na Keiki O Ka Moi 4

Iron Non-Koa Female

1	2.12.00	Koa Kai 6
2	2.12.16	West Coast Hakuna Matata
3	2.22.20	False Creek
4	2.25.26	Vernon Racing
5	2.26.47	Waikiki Beach Boys 3
6	2.29.32	Nakai E Walu 8
7	2.31.07	Kamehameha Oahu 1
8	2.32.06	Anuenue 1

Kapuna Female

1	2.39.09	Kai O Pua 9

Malia Female

1	2.15.54	Hanalei 2
2	2.16.00	Kai O Pua 7
3	2.20.49	Keauhou 6
4	2.36.08	North Shore

Masters Koa Female

1	2.06.43	Puna 3
2	2.22.29	Kai O Pua 5

Masters Non-Koa Female

1	2.10.42	Napili 3
2	2.14.42	Lokahi 7
3	2.20.36	Koloa
4	2.22.54	North Shore

Open Koa Female

1	1.57.04	Outrigger 3
2	2.10.22	Kai E Hitu 3
3	2.11.48	Anuenue 2
4	2.13.24	Koloa 2
5	2.13.42	Hanelei 1
6	2.14.35	Lae Ula O Kai Koa
7	2.17.35	Lanikai 2
8	2.21.21	Kona Athletic 1
9	2.21.59	Koa Kai 5
10	2.22.31	Nakai E Walu 7
1	2.23.21	Lokahi 6
12	2.25.07	Na Keiki O Ka Moi 2
13	2.25.57	Malama Ulu 1
14	2.28.13	Kawaihae 1

Open Non-Koa Female

1	1.57.06	Kailua 2
2	2.02.29	Kai O Pua 8
3	2.03.45	Lokahi 2
4	2.06.25	Hawaiian 1
5	2.07.04	Lanikai 1
6	2.07.44	Outrigger 4
7	2.08.26	Kailua 3
8	2.09.23	Kai E Hitu 2
9	2.10.53	Waikiki Surf 6
10	2.11.45	Lokahi 3
11	2.12.29	Marina Del Ray 3
12	2.13.11	Waikiki Surf 7
13	2.14.55	Puna 4
14	2.16.42	Napili 4
15	2.16.48	Lahaina 1
16	2.16.52	Keaukaha 1
17	2.16.55	Outrigger 7
18	2.17.32	Waikiki Surf 4
19	2.17.54	Waikoloa 1
20	2.18.56	Marianas Paddle Sports
21	2.21.09	Puuwai 4
22	2.21.28	Hanelei 3
23	2.23.34	Hawaiian 2
24	2.23.42	Hokuloa
25	2.23.51	Kamehamha 3
26	2.24.04	Kaiola 2
27	2.24.13	Lokahi 4
28	2.25.31	Hui O Sacramento
29	2.25.50	Waikiki Surf Club 5
30	2.25.56	Melama Ulu 3
31	2.26.14	Hui Nalu 2
32	2.26.43	Manu O Ke Kai 3

33	2.27.23	Lokahi 5
34	2.27.45	Lanikai 3
35	2.27.50	Columbia River
36	2.28.21	Marina Del Ray 2
37	2.30.48	Kamehameha Oahu 2
38	2.30.57	Koa Kai 4
39	2.31.36	Kai E Hitu 1
40	2.31.46	Waikiki Yacht 3
41	2.32.22	Pookela 3

Senior Masters Koa Female

1	2.24.58	Keoua 3

Senior Masters Non-Koa Female

1	2.22.46	Kai O Pua 6
2	2.28.31	Koa Kai 3

15-18 Male

1	2.36.18	Puuwai 3
2	2.36.28	Hawaiian 4
3	2.37.56	Hawaiian 3
4	2.39.57	Hui Nalu 3
5	2.45.46	Lokahi 12

Iron Koa Male

1	2.40.34	Malamu Ulu 5
2	2.47.12	Keoua 1
3	3.12.31	Lotus

Iron Masters Male

1	2.13.33	
2	2.21.38	Hanalei 6
3	2.22.27	Hui Lanakila 3
4	2.24.40	Keauhou 5
5	2.41.17	Imua
6	2.42.29	Lokahi
7	2.46.58	Lokahi 11
8	2.48.29	Keoua
9	2.55.20	Koa Kai 1
10	3.03.58	Hui Na Po'okela
		Nakai E Walu 4

Iron Non-Koa Male

1	2.23.28	Koloa
2	2.27.41	Tamarii Motu'uta
3	2.29.54	Hawaiian Canoe & Kayak 3
4	2.31.21	Koa Kai 8
5	2.31.45	Kawaihae 4
6	2.40.24	Waikiki Beach Boys
7	2.41.30	Vernon Racing 2
8	2.57.08	Keaukaha 3
9	2.58.13	Kilohana 1
10	3.01.04	American Swan Boat Team
11	3.29.19	Alapa Hoe

Iron Senior Masters Male

1	2.28.56	Great Lakes Brigade
2	2.44.20	Nakai E Walu 3
3	2.56.41	Keauhou 3
4	3.00.08	Malama Ulu 2
5	3.18.13	Kilohana 2

Kupuna Male

1	2.53.20	Keauhou 4
2	3.01.16	Kai O Pua 1
3	3.06.15	Lanikai 8

Malia Male

1	2.38.02	Kai E Hitu 4
2	2.38.57	Hanelei 4
3	2.40.13	Keauhou 3
4	2.45.59	Kai O Pua 2
5	3.03.21	Keauhou

6	3.11.05	Lanikai 9

Masters Koa Male

1	2.30.23	Puna 1
2	2.33.33	Waikiki Yacht 4
3	2.56.30	Kai E Hitu 7

Masters Non-Koa Male

1	2.11.41	Outrigger 5
2	2.19.14	Kanaka Ikaika 1
3	2.20.37	Malama Ulu 6
4	2.25.41	Lokahi 8
5	2.32.19	Puuwai 1
6	2.32.43	Hawaiian 8
7	2.34.18	Kehei
8	2.42.22	Kaipoha
9	2.45.52	Windward Kai

Open Koa Male

1	2.02.39	Lanikai 5
2	2.09.29	Kai E Hitu 5
3	2.11.52	Outrigger 1
4	2.22.24	Kai O Pua 4
5	2.36.51	Na Keiki O Ka Moi 1
6	2.39.06	Kamehamha 1
7	2.55.11	Lae Ula O Kai 1

Open Non-Koa Male

1	2.03.20	Outrigger 2
2	2.05.40	Waikiki Surf 3
3	2.09.20	Hawaiian 7
4	2.10.26	Lanikai 6
5	2.11.02	Waikiki Beach Boys 2
6	2.11.16	Hawaiian Canoe & Kayak 2
7	2.12.25	Kai O Pua 3
8	2.12.32	Hawaiian
9	2.14.14	Puuwai 2
10	2.14.42	Hui Lanakila 1
11	2.15.25	Kailua 4
12	2.15.46	Waikiki Surf 2
13	2.17.26	Lokahi 9
14	2.17.54	Waikiki Beach Boys 1
15	2.19.23	Healani 1
16	2.22.26	Anuenue 3
17	2.26.19	Kamehamha 2
18	2.26.41	Hoopili
19	2.27.44	Napili 2
20	2.30.06	Kailua 6
21	2.30.24	Malama Ulu 4
22	2.31.12	Nakai E Walu 1
23	2.31.26	Kona Athletic 2
24	2.31.50	Manu O Ke Kai 1
25	2.32.03	Marianas Paddle Sports 2
26	2.32.32	Kailua 5
27	2.33.22	Hui Lanakila 2
28	2.34.22	Waikiki Yacht 1
29	2.34.47	Kahana
30	2.35.19	Waikiki Surf 1
31	2.36.39	Pookela 2
32	2.37.17	Kalihi Kai
33	2.37.37	Lokahi 10
34	2.37.49	Puna
35	2.38.04	Napili 1
36	2.38.33	Koa Kai 7
37	2.39.26	Waikiki Yacht 2
38	2.39.51	Pili Hawaiian Hoe
39	2.39.59	Lanikai 4

40	2.40.58	Lanikai 7	2	2.29.28	Anuenue 4
41	2.41.22	Na Keiki O Ka Moi 3	**Senior Masters Non-Koa Male**		
42	2.41.34	Kai Elua/Honohono	1	2.16.19	Hanelei 7
43	2.44.00	Healani 2	2	2.39.17	Kailua 1
44	2.46.16	Hanalei 5	3	2.44.29	Keauhou 2
45	2.46.41	Keahiakahoe	4	2.44.48	Keaukaha 2
46	2.46.57	Kaiola 1	5	2.48.00	Kai E Hitu 6
47	2.48.02	Marina Del Ray 1	6	2.48.21	Manu O Ke Kai 2
48	2.56.51	Koa Kai 9	7	2.48.40	Outrigger 6
Senior Masters Koa Male			8	2.57.18	Koa Kai 2
1	2.23.17	Kona Athletic			

Na Wahini O Ke Kai Molokai, September 1995

1	5.24.42	Offshore 1	Open	Non-Koa	California
2	5.31.09	Outrigger 1	Open	Non-Koa	Oahu
3	5.36.00	Kailua 1	Open	Non-Koa	Oahu
4	5.41.04	Lanakila 1	Open	Non-Koa	California
5	5.41.54	Kai Opua 1	Open	Non-Koa	Hawaii /Big Island
6	5.42.54	Lokahi 1	Open	Non-Koa	Oahu
7	5.43.22	Umbi Gumbi	Open	Non-Koa	Australia
8	5.48.18	Outrigger 2	Open	Non-Koa	Oahu
9	5.51.43	Waikiki Surf 1	Open	Koa	Oahu
10	5.53.51	Maui Master	Master		Maui
11	5.54.32	Hawaiian 1	Open	Non-Koa	Maui
12	5.54.51	Koa Kai 1	Open	Non-Koa	Oahu
13	5.57.37	Kailua 2	Open	Koa	Oahu
14	5.58.10	Kai Opua	Open	Non-Koa	Hawaii/Big Island
15	5.58.34	Hanalei	Open	Non-Koa	Kauai
16	5.59.25	Waikiki Surf 2	Open	Non-Koa	Oahu
17	5.59.33	Maui Jim	Open	Non-Koa	Maui
18	5.59.53	Lanikai 1	Open	Non-Koa	Oahu
19	6.00.00	Koloa	Open	Non-Koa	Kauai
20	6.01.30	Lokahi Masters	Master	Non-Koa	Oahu
21	6.02.28	Offshore 2	Open	Koa	California
22	6.02.55	Dana Point	Open	Non-Koa	California
23	6.03.30	Puna	Open	Non-Koa	Hawaii/Big Island
24	6.04.26	Outrigger Australia	Open	Non-Koa	Australia
25	6.05.29	Anuenue	Open	Non-Koa	Oahu
26	6.08.12	Lokahi 2	Open	Non-Koa	Oahu
27	6.09.20	Kahakai	Master	Non-Koa	California
28	6.12.33	Keauhou Masters	Master	Non-Koa	Hawaii/Big Island
29	6.12.46	Puuwai	Open	Non-Koa	Kuai
30	6.13.58	Law Ula O Kai	Open	Non-Koa	Maui
31	6.14.30	Kai Opua Masters	Master	Non-Koa	Hawaii/Big Island
32	6.16.43	Waikiki Surf 3	Open	Non-Koa	Oahu
33	6.18.17	North Shore Masters	Master	Non-Koa	Oahu
34	6.18.20	Kamehameha (Hilo)	Open	Non-Koa	Hawaii/Big Island
35	6.19.18	Napili	Open	Non-Koa	Maui
36	6.19.30	Lanakila 2	Open	Koa	California
37	6.20.09	Na Kai Ewalu	Open	Non-Koa	Oahu
38	6.20.34	Lokahi	Open	Non-Koa	Oahu
39	6.20.56	Manu O Ke Kai	Open	Non-Koa	Oahu
40	6.21.36	Cenral Oregon	Open	Non-Koa	Oregon
41	6.21.37	Lanikai 2	Open	Koa	Oahu
42	6.24.01	Koa Kai Sr Masters	Senior Master	Non-Koa	Oahu
43	6.24.13	Honolulu	Open	Koa	Oahu
44	6.28.36	Hawaiian 2	Open	Non-Koa	Maui
45	6.30.56	Koa Kai 2	Open	Non-Koa	Oahu
46	6.33.40	Hui Nalu	Open	Non-Koa	Oahu
47	6.37.58	Kihei	Open	Koa	Maui
48	6.38.03	Kai Poha	Open	Non-Koa	Oahu

Bankoh Moloka'i Hoe / Moloka'i, October 1995

1	4.53.03.00	Lanikai 1	Open	Non-Koa	Oahu
2	5.01.39.16	Faa'a	Open	Non-Koa	Tahiti
3	5.03.00.40	Outrigger 1	Open	Non-Koa	Oahu
4	5.09.08.67	Waikiki Surf 1	Open	Non-Koa	Oahu
5	5.10.56.99	Outrigger Australia	Open	Non-Koa	Australia
6	5.13.27.61	Dana Point 1	Open	Non-Koa	California
7	5.15.42.45	Hawaii Canoe & Kayak	Open	Non-Koa	Oahu
8	5.17.09.59	Waikiki Beach Boys 1	Open	Non-Koa	Oahu
10*	5.19.48.62	Mooloolaba	Masters	Non-Koa	Australia
11	5.20.09.79	Lanakila 1	Open	Non-Koa	California
12	5.21.54.08	Kai Opua	Open	Non-Koa	Hawaii
9*	5.25.15.24	Hawaiian 1	Open	Non-Koa	Maui
13	5.27.01.65	Outrigger 3	Masters	Non-Koa	Oahu
14	5.28.06.14	Hawaiian 2	Open	Non-Koa	Maui
15	5.28.27.03	Hui Lanakila 2	Open	Non-Koa	Oahu
16	5.30.24.50	Lokahi 1	Open	Non-Koa	Oahu
17	5.30.55.49	Hamilton Island	Open	Non-Koa	Australia
18	5.32.23.84	Marina Del Rey	Open	Non-Koa	California
19	5.33.06.13	Lanikai 2	Open	Non-Koa	Oahu
20	5.35.36.56	Hui Lanakila 1	Open	Non-Koa	Oahu
21	5.36.223.42	Outrigger 2	Open	Koa	Oahu
22	5.38.40.03	Malama Ula 2	Masters	Non-Koa	Maui
23	5.39.13.85	Waikiki Surf 2	Open	Non-Koa	Oahu
24	5.40.23.04	Tui Tonga	Masters	Non-Koa	Tonga
25	5.40.49.35	Puna	Masters	Non-Koa	Hawaii
26	5.41.43.41	Tiger Canoe & Kayak	Open	Non-Koa	Hawaii
27	5.42.12.85	Napili 1	Open	Non-Koa	Maui
28	5.44.19.01	Nike Hungary	Open	Non-Koa	Hungary
29	5.46.42.66	Waikiki Beach Boys	Open	Non-Koa	Oahu
30	5.47.12.01	Anuenue 2	Senior Masters	Non-Koa	Oahu
31	5.47.24.06	Lanikai 3	Open	Non-Koa	Oahu
32	5.47.57.01	Keahiakahoe	Open	Non-Koa	Oahu
33	5.48.24.83	Pu'uwai 1	Open	Non-Koa	Kauai
34	5.49.14.93	Anuenue 1	Open	Non-Koa	Oahu
35	5.49.23.31	Kona Athletic 1	Open	Non-Koa	Hawaii
36	5.49.23.97	Kailua 5	Senior Masters	Non-Koa	Oahu
37	5.50.17.03	Keauhou 1	Masters	Non-Koa	Hawaii
38	5.51.03.32	False Creek	Open	Non-Koa	Canada
39	5.51.19.11	Waikiki Surf 3	Open	Non-Koa	Oahu
40	5.51.58.41	Dana Point 2	Senior Masters	Non-Koa	California
41	5.52.05.37	Lanakila 2	Open	Koa	California
42	5.52.41.46	Kahana	Open	Non-Koa	Maui
43	5.53.37.59	Napili 2	Open	Non-Koa	Maui
45	5.54.36.86	Outrigger Whitsunday	Masters	Non-Koa	Australia
46	5.56.00.69	Hawaiian 3	Masters	Non-Koa	Maui
47	5.56.06.80	Jericho Outrigger	Open	Non-Koa	Canada
48	5.57.48.05	Northcliff Australia	Open	Non-Koa	Australia
49	5.58.41.46	Koa Kai 1	Open	Non-Koa	Oahu
50	5.59.58.25	Manuiwa	Masters	Non-Koa	New England
51	6.00.15.14	Waikiki Beach Boys 3	Open	Non-Koa	Oahu
52	6.01.38.57	Healani 1	Open	Non-Koa	Oahu
53	6.03.00.49	Koa Kai 3	Masters	Non-Koa	Oahu
54	6.03.55.44	Koolau	Open	Non-Koa	Oahu
55	6.04.54.77	Lokahi 3	Masters	Non-Koa	Oahu
56	6.06.03.55	Waikiki Yacht 1	Open	Non-Koa	Oahu
57	6.06.52.75	Kilua 3	Open	Non-Koa	Oahu
58	6.07.04.02	Pu'Uwai 2	Masters	Non-Koa	Kauai
59	6.08.50.50	Kamehameha (Hilo)	Open	Non-Koa	Hawaii
60	6.09.06.36	Honolulu 1	Open	Non-Koa	Oahu
61	6.10.40.29	Lokahi 2	Open	Non-Koa	Oahu
62	6.11.38.92	Waikiki Yacht 3	Masters	Non-Koa	Oahu

63	6.14.57.87	Lanikai 4	Open	Koa	Oahu
64	6.15.58.02	Kailua 4	Open	Non-Koa	Oahu
65	6.17.19.83	Kamehameha (Oahu)	Open	Non-Koa	Oahu
66	6.18.40.03	Kalama Ohana	Open	Non-Koa	Molokai
67	6.19.59.90	Keauhou 2	Senior Masters	Non-Koa	Hawaii
68	6.20.45.61	Na Kai Ewala 1	Senior Masters	Non-Koa	Maui
69	6.21.09.83	Malama Ula 1	Open	Non-Koa	Maui
70	6.21.55.02	Hui Nalu 1	Open	Koa	Oahu
71	6.22.04.21	Waikiki Yacht 2	Open	Non-Koa	Oahu
72	6.22.11.66	Kai Poha	Open	Non-Koa	Oahu
73	6.25.04.06	Kona Athletic 2	Senior Masters	Koa	Hawaii
74	6.27.00.06	Na Kai Ewalu 2	Senior Masters	Non-Koa	Maui
75	6.27.07.32	Alapa Hoe	Open	Non-Koa	Oahu
76	6.27.28.92	Kihei	Open	Koa	Maui
77	6.27.30.57	Taniwha Grizzles	Masters	Non-Koa	New England
78	6.30.12.27	Lae Ula O Kai	Open	Non-Koa	Maui
79	6.33.59.20	Koa Kai 2	Open	Non-Koa	Oahu
80	6.36.53.20	Hui Nalu 2	Senior Masters	Non-Koa	Oahu
81	6.39.38.78	Johnson Island Ekahi	Open	Non-Koa	Johnson Island
82	6.39.54.01	Kalihi Kai	Open	Non-Koa	Oahu
83	6.40.48.28	Kai E Hitu	Senior Masters	Non-Koa	Hawaii
84	6.40.53.54	Johnson Island Elua	Open	Non-Koa	Johnson Island
85	6.44.21.30	Lanikai 6	Senior Masters	Non-Koa	Oahu
86	6.51.30.37	Lanikai 5	Masters	Non-Koa	Oahu
87	6.52.12.18	Healani 2	Open	Non-Koa	Oahu
88	7.13.29.35	Honolulu 2	Senior Masters	Non-Koa	Oahu

Hawaiki Nui Va'a - Tahiti, November 1995

Stage1	Stage 2	Stage 3	Total Time	Total Points	Crew	Locallity
3.44.00	1.24.51	3.57.49	9.06.40	8	Fare Ara	ISLV
4.04.29	1.27.51	3.54.46	9.27.06	23	As Havai	ISLV
3.58.17	1.30.23	4.08.03	9.36.43	38	Tahaa Nui	ISLV
4.13.37	1.26.13	4.01.22	9.41.12	38	As Tamarii Erai	Australia
3.56.13	1.28.31	4.19.36	9.44.20	44	As Hinaraurea	ISLV
4.12.24	1.31.00	4.09.57	9.53.21	58	As Tepaetia Pir	Tuamotu
4.05.39	1.32.14	4.22.06	9.59.59	72	Rautoa Nui	ISLV
4.12.05	1.33.09	4.17.38	10.02.52	78	As Kua Moehau	Marquesas
4.09.53	1.34.27	4.10.02	9.54.22	80	Te Ava Rua	ISLV
4.12.17	1.33.15	4.19.58	10.05.30	83	Punamoe	ISLV
4.23.18	1.31.38	4.14.29	10.09.25	87	As Tam Arutai	ISLV
4.19.52	1.32.20	4.19.44	10.11.56	92	As Ha'Avai	ISLV
4.21.00	1.33.36	4.16.14	10.10.50	98	Terere A Fara	ISLV
4.22.12	1.32.50	4.22.24	10.17.26	106	Tetaharoa Tahaa	ISLV
4.32.57	1.31.24	4.24.03	10.28.24	111	As Havai	ISLV
4.06.14	1.34.01	4.40.29	10.20.44	112	As Hei Mataiki	Marquesas
4.21.31	1.37.19	4.15.48	10.14.38	119	Boranuivaaa	ISLV
4.22.05	1.39.44	4.16.28	10.18.17	126	As Tere A Tia Hoe	ISLV
4.17.32	1.35.07	4.29.05	10.21.44	127	Te Tai Rapatia	ISLV
4.20.26	1.34.18	4.33.07	10.27.51	131	Tamarii Faaroa	ISLV
4.17.46	1.37.37	4.27.28	10.22.51	136	As Faaaha Nui	ISLV
4.29.12	1.35.36	4.23.14	10.28.02	138	As Farerama	ISLV
4.39.58	1.35.55	4.25.41	10.41.34	152	As Rainui Tahaa	ISLV
4.46.29	1.43.03	4.38.09	11.07.41	177	As Pir De Hao	Tuamotu
4.44.07	1.38.23	4.43.16	11.05.46	178	As Tamarii Uporu	ISLV
4.33.35	1.30.53	0.00.00	6.04.28	999	CMSA Moruroa	Tuamotu
CORPORATE TEAMS						
4.05.57	1.30.11	4.07.06	9.43.14	41		Uscan
4.16.25	1.34.43	4.17.12	10.08.20	101		Mobil
4.13.01	1.33.53	4.25.26	10.12.20	103		Tamarii Socredo
33.44	1.36.27	4.21.12	10.31.23	138		Air Tahiti

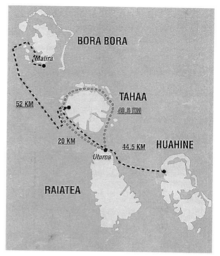

This event takes place in the Leeward Islands northwest of the island of Tahiti with paddlers departing from Huahine, crossing Raiatea (the sacred) lagoon and Tahaa to end up on the majestic island of Bora Bora. This open ocean iron marathon event was founded in 1992 when thirty-four canoes competed.

The event consists of three stages over three days, totalling one hundred and sixteen kilometres. This year, sixty-four starters lined up for the first stage and by day three there were also four hundred and twenty-five other craft accompanying the paddlers.

Of the sixty-four starters, only two failed to complete all three stages and, as it was in 1994, of those in the first twenty overall placings ten were from Tahiti and ten from others islands. Amongst regulars in the top twenty were Fare Are, Havai, Tamarii Erai and Hinaraurea from the other islands. A team's overall rating is calculated by adding the points gained for each of the three stages.

RECORDS TO BEAT:

Stage one	Te Ui Va'a	1994	3.23.10
Stage two	Te Ui Va'a	1994	1.20.01
Stage three	Faa'a	1993	3.48.39.
Overall	Faa'a	1993	8.43.14.

PLACE GETTERS OVER PREVIOUS YEARS:

1992 – Faa'a, Te U'I Va'a and Rautere

1993 – Faa'a, Te U'I Va'a and Fareara

1994 – Te U'I Va'a 1, Faa'a and Fareara.

If you would like to find out more please contact: As Comite Organisateur Hawaiki Nui Va'a PO Box 20 846 - 98713, Papeete RP, Tahiti, French Polynesia. Phone (689) 42 9767, 42 6317, Fax (689) 42 1466.

PRIZE MONEY $50,000 PRIZE MONEY

Hamilton Cup
June 14 - 17 1996

Get amongst the winners at Australia's premier Outrigger Canoeing event.

Enjoy *Coca-Cola* TRADE MARK REGD

HAMILTON ISLAND GREAT BARRIER REEF
Holiday Inn CROWNE PLAZA RESORT

XXXX **Our beer.**

ANSETT AUSTRALIA

Last Year's Winners

Open Men
Outrigger Australia — $6000
Panamuna — $3000
Hawaiian Canoe & Kayak Team — $1000

Open Women
Panamuna — $6000
Sydney — $3000
Hamilton Island — $1000

Master Men
Mooloolaba — $6000
Team Hawaii — $3000
Imua California — $1000

Master Women
Capricorn Coast — $6000
Brisbane — $3000
Surfers Paradise — $1000

Surf Ski Classic
Dean Gardiner — $6000
Ian Rowlings — $3000
Adam Morley — $1000

Televised Australia Wide by Channel Nine's Wide World of Sport

HAMILTON ISLAND OUTRIGGER CANOE CLUB

For Further Information contact Gaye Dolahenty on (079) 468 797

PRIZE MONEY $50,000 PRIZE MONEY

Hamilton Cup
AUSTRALIA 1995

A crew from Hamilton Island Outrigger Canoe Club greets the replica barque *Young Endeavour*, named after Captain James Cook's exploratory vessel *Endeavour* which sailed into this region in June 1770. A scene such as this would have been common throughout the Pacific region, with visiting ships stopping for supplies often being greeted by thousands of outrigger canoe paddlers in their canoes. Photo: Barry Alsop

From the outset, the 1995 Hamilton Cup was always going to be a bit different from previous years. For the first time in the sport of outrigger canoe racing, substantial prize money was on offer – courtesy of Coca-Cola, as part of a five year A$250,000 deal.

This investment in outrigger canoe racing is a sign that, in Australia at any rate, the sport has what it takes to sell products in the nineties. Its ethnic, healthy, dynamic image is just the *right thing* to associate with. One can only speculate to what degree Coke will further reinforce that link in the future. TV commercials featuring canoes and paddlers battling the high seas, followed by scenes on a sun-drenched beach, where paddlers, exhausted yet elated, reach into ice buckets for cans. Pulling on the rings and snapping them to lips in one motion, we share a big fat close-up of the moment when the refreshing liquid explodes on the backs of throats. But, I digress!

Of A$50,000 prize money $40,000 was allocated to the main event the 42.2km marathon. The remaining $10,000 was distributed between two surf ski events, both won by Australian Dean Gardiner, winner of the Bankoh Kayak Challenge (Moloka'i to Hawaii Kai, 51.49km, 32 miles) and the 1992, '93 and '94 record holder.

Now doubtless there will be those amongst us who will view this monetary reward thing as a little hard to stomach. After all aren't we on the brink of

Harbourside at Hamilton. Docking spot for mainland barges freighting canoes, paddlers and spectators Thursday until Saturday. With each arrival the atmosphere builds. One hundred and twenty crews - seven hundred and twenty paddlers - made this the biggest event so far in its twelve year history. Photo: Barry Alsop

professionalism here? Well, yes perhaps this is so, but this feature is really not concerned with the ethics of things, or a debate about whether we should be cautious about taking this direction.

What we can say, is that international competition, is only international by degree – the degree to which other nations participate. Does one, two, or even three overseas teams constitute an international event? In order for a budding international event to attract greater numbers of overseas participants, monetary prizes tend to sweeten the bitter pill of travel expenses. You've got to be in it to win it. Monetary incentive will attract the gun crews as it is beginning to in Tahiti with the Hawaiki Nui race. So the event benefits further by greater competition, media attention and therefore exposure.

WITH THIS IN MIND, THE HAMILTON CUP IS SURE TO GROW AS ONE OF THE WORLD'S PREMIER OUTRIGGER EVENTS, AS THE NEWS SPREADS THAT SUBSTANTIAL PRIZE MONEY IS ON OFFER. USA TEAMS FROM HAWAII AND CALIFORNIA TOOK AWAY A TOTAL OF A$7,000 IN THE OUTRIGGER DIVISION AND $1,000 IN THE SURF SKI EVENT.

OUT OF THE ONE HUNDRED AND TWENTY CREWS PARTICIPATING, THE FIVE OVERSEAS TEAMS (THREE FROM HAWAII AND TWO FROM CALIFORNIA) AND THREE INDIVIDUALS WHO PADDLED WITH MOOLOOLABA MASTERS, WON (AND ASSISTED IN WINNING) A TOTAL OF NINETEEN MEDALS OUT OF SIXTY-THREE IN BOTH SIX-PERSON AND SOLO DIVISIONS. THIS REPRESENTS OVER THIRTY PERCENT OF THE POSSIBLE HAUL, BY ONLY SIX PERCENT OF THE TOTAL NUMBER OF PADDLERS!

With ever increasing participation by top crews from Hawaii, California, New Zealand and Tahiti, more of the money stands a chance of leaving Australia; proof positive that the Hamilton Cup is a genuine

Above: OCC Hawaii open ladies adding to the international flavour of Hamilton '95. Photos Barry Alsop

Da boyz from Hawaiian Canoe Kayak.

Hawaiian Canoe Kayak Team turning at the 1000m mark on the way to winning their 2000m final.

international event attracting the best teams from around the world.

Overseas teams included those from Hawaii – an open ladies' crew from Outrigger Canoe Club and a master crew; Team Hawaii Masters and three master men individuals also from OCC who paddled with 1994 Moloka'i winners Mooloolaba; and also a men's crew from Hawaiian Canoe Kayak Team. From California, master men and master ladies from Imua, Newport Beach.

Their participation was for me, what made the Hamilton Cup 1995 especially memorable. Their numbers were just enough to create that international flavour making it stand out from your average race meet. What was particularly interesting was their reaction to seeing Australian outrigging in action and the news isn't all good. They were amazed particularly at the way in which some crews treated their equipment with canoes dragged nose first up the beach, equipment tossed on the ground and paddles jammed into the sand; treated as if they were of little value, either materially or spiritually. "We don't see things like this in Hawaii or California", was the general observation. Sponsorship certainly warps some paddlers perspective of the value of equipment it would seem.

That aside, the racing was as you would expect, highly competitive. Held over four days beginning on Friday with the solo division events, 500m sprints and 8km (women) and 9.6km marathons. Conditions for the sprints were blustery with a strong south easterly wind creating a few bumps along the course.

The marathon events held later in the

Start of the Women's 16.1km marathon. Windy start conditions tested the crews in the early stage of the race as they jostled for positions.

Action during the Open Women's 2000m Sprint final, Panamuna in foreground.

day were also in blustery conditions and many of the ladies found their altered course, starting and finishing from the beach at Catseye Bay, hard going as they struggled against strong currents on the return leg. This is certainly one feature of racing around the waters of Hamilton Island, the strong currents and tidal range. Some felt they were going backwards part of the time.

Central to the solo events was the introduction by Canoe Sports Australia of the Ocean Master solo canoe which won the majority of medals on the day and looks set to do much for the expansion of this division in Australia, being a robust, well-designed, ocean-going craft.

During Friday a steady procession of people had been arriving so that by Saturday morning the number of paddlers had swelled considerably. Whilst the weather had been sunny and blustery on the first day, Saturday's forecast wasn't great.

The master men's 16.1km around-the-island marathon began Saturday morning in reasonably horrendous conditions out from the beach at Catseye Bay. In the passage the tide was raging and a strong wind against it was creating some challenging standing waves, which proved too much for several crews who flipped moments after the start; one team failed to get going again.

Later in the day the first of the six-person 2000m master's sprints began. As always this produced some tight racing over the 500m course which, with three

Photo: Barry Alsop

Team Hawaii Masters (above) and Mooloolaba Masters (below) - South Head waters.

turns, saw positions change at practically every turn. As a casual observation, many crews have much to learn about making turns around buoys which they were able to see for themselves by watching the Hawaiian and Californian crews.

By the end of day two, the event seemed fully under way, with practically all of the seven hundred and twenty competitors now on the island and the atmosphere building.

Sunday saw the open and master women's 16.1km marathon start in sunny, windy conditions. The passage had calmed quiet considerably from the day before and all canoes got off to a clean start except for a few directional problems encountered by some of the less experienced steerers as they got into the strong current of the Passage.

Local knowledge plays a big part in the course taken by steerers and doing your homework definitely pays off at this event. Talking to locals and your own shrewd assessment of the course are essential to good results in this event.

Evenings at the Barefoot Bar were definitely getting livelier. The usual excessive consumption and unusual behaviour beginning to peak. With the promise of rain, strong winds and a 42.2km race on the following morning, the partying stopped almost as soon as it had started except for those who had not enrolled in that particular form of punishment.

MONDAY'S BIG MARATHON IS UNDOUBTEDLY THE

MAIN EVENT AND A FITTING CLIMAX TO THE HAMILTON CUP. WHERE THE OTHER EVENTS ARE THE ENTREE, THIS IS THE MAIN COURSE. THE RULES ALLOW FOR CREWS OF TEN WOMEN AND NINE MEN AND AS ALWAYS SPECULATION WAS RIFE AS TO THE FAVOURED CREWS.

In the open women's division, Australian club Panamuna had not been beaten throughout the club season. With past Commonwealth and Olympic swimmer Lisa Curry-Kenny devoting herself full time to outrigger canoeing (in the role of captain and coach) the team had the direction, focus and commitment to give it their all, especially as they had not won this event previously.

Defending champions and course record holders Sydney OCC, train almost exclusively for this premier event. Sydney's geographic isolation from much of the rest of the outrigging strongholds throughout Australia means that their training is very much in the dark in terms of knowing how they compare. With a new canoe, they certainly went into the event full of confidence, knowing that Panamuna would be the crew to beat.

Hamilton Island ladies were all fired up and with local knowledge on their side, they knew that what they lacked in fitness

and strength, they could make up on the way around. The 1995 crew were considered the strongest of any past Hamilton ladies crews.

Outrigger Hawaii certainly hadn't come to have a gentle cruise around the course. With all their fund raising efforts and training to get to Hamilton they were also ready to give it their best, along with other strong crews such as Brisbane with several world class kayak paddlers in the crew.

From the men's perspective, Outrigger Australia were back to defend their title and as the winner of this event more times than any other club, they are always going to be a hard crew to beat. As Ian Rowlings commented prior to the race, their greatest strength is in their depth of talent – some twenty paddlers competing for nine places making for a strong crew. Despite most of them being as he described *"no names"*, their crew comprised some very talented and dedicated outrigger canoe paddlers.

Panamuna men, captained by Grant Kenny, consisted largely of the 1994 crew with a few new inclusions, such as world class surf-ski paddler Dean Gardiner and Tahitian paddler Lois Laughlin.

Grant felt they were the "best prepared"

Mooloolaba Masters change-over in Dent Passage.

Panamuna Men's crew held the lead until just after South Head when defending champions Outrigge Australia overtook them on the critical leg to Pentecost Island. Photo: Barry Alsop

crew he had been with, but the fact remained that some of the crew had not spent much, if any, time training together, which was also the problem for the Hawaiian Canoe Kayak Team, who had recruited two of Hawaii's strongest paddlers, the Foti brothers.

Jim Foti understood this potential *dial-a-crew* problem straight away and made it clear that although he knew they had the manpower and the skill it would depend how soon they could get the team working together.

The master men's division was also going to be a battle, with the likes of Californian champions Imua masters, Team Hawaii Masters steered by Tom Connor, and the Mooloolaba master crew with invitation paddlers Mike Fox, Walter Guild and steerer Todd Bradley of Outrigger Hawaii. Northcliffe masters, arch rivals with Mooloolaba on the race circuit, were also going to give it their all.

It was something of a mystery how the master ladies would perform, with many of the crews relying on ring-ins from other crews to get the numbers.

Rather like going on holiday, the pre-

arrangements and the journey itself are often half the fun and so is the speculation and preparation prior to a race of this proportion. Once the race is underway, the time for talk ends and so much of what was said dissolves like aspirin in water, cloudy at first, but soon clearing to reveal the truth.

The morning was windy, gloomy and wet and a hard race was a certainty. Down at harbourside, crews, full of anticipation. had been checking rigging, taping down covers, consuming fluids, stuffing carbo's and making ready from almost the time the sun had risen, or tried to rise. By the time the fifty-nine crews were on the start line it was pouring, visibility was limited, but the passage quite calm. That is until the other side of Dent Island.

Panamuna men reached the southern tip of Dent Island first followed closely by Outrigger Australia . Panamuna women had also established a lead over OCC Hawaii and Sydney.

THE FIRST CHANGE-OVER IS NOT ALLOWED UNTIL CANOES REACH THE LIGHTHOUSE AROUND THE TOP END OF DENT, AND BY THIS STAGE THE FIELD HAD SPLIT CONSIDERABLY. HERE THE WATER WAS ROUGH AND THE CHANGE-OVER WAS CRUCIAL FOR ALL CREWS. SUPPORT

In this sequence at South Head, Team Hawaii Masters in the foreground is being overtaken by Mooloolaba Masters. The first frame shows the exit of the Mooloolaba stroke with numbers two and four. Frame two, relief paddlers entering. In frame three, Team Hawaii Masters' number two also exits. Fantastic action in genuine rough water paddling conditions.

Team Hawaii Masters ran into problems at the first change when their support boat didn't show bu managed however to hold their division lead until South Head. The rough conditions meant that man support boats ran into problems.

BOATS, TOSSING IN CHAOTIC WATERS SEARCHED FOR CANOES; OFTEN DIFFICULT IN THE RAIN. AS CANOES APPROACHED AND BOATS FOUND THEIR CREWS THE CHANGE-OVERS CAME THICK AND FAST.

Team Hawaii Masters ran into problems immediately as they had lost their support boat and continued without a change for another 2-3km and continued the race with little support.

Panamuna established a 100 metre lead on Outrigger by Dent Passage. Outrigger hugged to Dent Island hoping to use the current to advantage, Panamuna crossed to the Hamilton side. By the time they reached South Head, Outrigger was a boat length ahead. Panamuna managed to pull back and over take, then made a change and bailed which allowed Outrigger to pass and at that point they pushed ahead, with Panamuna working hard to play catch up.

THE STRETCH TO PENTECOST ISLAND IS THE MAKE OR BREAK PART OF THE RACE. A GOOD LEAD HERE SETS YOU UP FOR A FAST HOME LEG WITH A FOLLOWING SEA AND WIND. PADDLERS KNOW THIS AND IN THIS RESPECT IT CONSTITUTES A LARGE PART OF THE RACE.

Outrigger Australia, winners of this event more than any other club. This time $6000 better off. Photo Barry Alsop

Panamuna Open Women. Photo Barry Alsop

South head claimed a few victims with its usual nasty self. Panamuna ladies arrived here first and were unchallenged for the rest of the race. The Hamilton Island crew and Sydney toughed it out for second and third, with Sydney eventually overtaking.

Sore butts, sore guts, raw hands, bumps and bruises and stories of adventure were enchanged at race end. Hamilton '95 was a harsh race; rough, wet and windy but outrigger canoe racing thrives on hardship and teamwork. Tough conditions only serve to bring paddlers closer together. Long after the physical and mental wounds have healed, memories of a confrontation with nature's most powerful elements will serve to sustain us in our artificially comfortable world – in this case the Barefoot Bar. While some partied long into the night, others slept, but most agreed they would be back in '96.

Keith Williams (right) founder of the Hamilton Cup and one of the driving forces behind the introduction of outrigger canoe racing into Australia, at the awards ceremony. Photo Barry Alsop

Helgeson's images in the Hawaiian Outrigger Canoe Paddling

series celebrate the regatta scene. From his original oils,

watercolors and grahite drawings, some works are available

in two sizes of limited edition giclée iris prints, while others

are offered as lithograph fine art posters.

RAYMOND HELGESON
F I N E   A R T

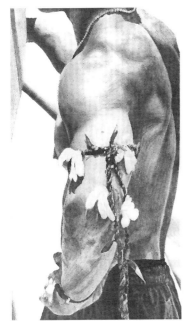

"PLUMERIA TI LEAF LEI"
©1991, b/w lithograph 15x11 inches $18

"PULLING WATER"
©1994, b/w lithograph 15x11 inches $18

"FOUR DETERMINED PADDLERS"
©1995, color lithograph 18x24 inches $36

Be sure and visit

HELGESON'S

ON LINE

ART

GALLERY

featuring his canoe paddling images.

http://www.maui.net/~helgeson/

157

"BLACK SAND BEACH PADDLERS"
©1993, edition of ninety giclée iris prints
24 x 16 inches $375
12 x 8 inches $190

"AFTER THE RACE"
©1994, edition of ninety giclée iris prints
24 x 16 inches $375
12 x 8 inches $190

HOW TO ORDER

Prices listed are in US dollars.
Send cheque or money order in US dollars, or foreign equivalent – plus
shipping and handling fees to:

Order total		Raymond Helgeson
$12 – $50	add $5	PO Box 383628
$51 – $100	add $10	Waikoloa
over $100	add 10%	Hawaii 96738 USA
		808 334-3330
		email: helgeson@maui.net

NEW EIGHT NOTE CARDS

OF FOUR POPULAR HELGESON IMAGES

INTO THE SURF

BLACK SAND
BEACH PADDLERS

AFTER THE RACE

FOUR DETERMINED
PADDLERS

Each purchase contains eight color cards and envelopes.

cpn 3   INTO THE SURF

cpn 5   AFTER THE RACE

cpn 6   BLACK SAND BEACH PADDLERS

cpn 7   FOUR DETERMINED PADDLERS

cpn A   Variety package – two cards of each.

"INTO THE SURF" ©1992, edition of ninety giclée iris prints
16 x 24 inches $375, 8 x 12 inches $190

Looking out over the famous calm seas of Kona to fluffy clouds on the horizon.

Queen Lili'uokalani
Kona Coast - Big Island Hawaii, September 1995

1996 Queen Lilioukalani August 31 - September 1
The 25th Anniversary!
Kai Opua Outrigger Canoe Club PO Box 3079 Kailua-Kona 96740

The spirit of Queen Lili'oukalani lives on as depicted in this poster by Eddy Y created especially for the event which is in her honour as the last reignning monarch of the Hawaiian Islands.

I had been told for some time about this event. About the friendship and atmosphere, about the unique mix of participants and above all about the spirit of *aloha* that prevails during the weekend. So, I went there to experience it . . . and I'm going back.

The venue is the small town of Kailua on the Kona coast of Hawaii, The Big Island. Host club is Kai Opua which stages the event from where the club is located at the front of the King Kamehameha Kona Beach Hotel.

This is a pictorial essay and a tribute to a special event.

Kona Kai 'Opua

Ha'a-he-o, I-ka ma-li-e
O Kona Kai 'o-pua i-ka-la-i
Ki-la-ki-la o, Hu-a-la-la-i
I ke ka ma-li-no a o Kona
Ha-no-ha-no
O Ko-na kai 'o-pua i ka la-i
Opu-a hi-na-no kau i la ma-li-e
Pu-a'i na wai
I ka maka o kai 'opua
A-o-le no
He lu-a a e li-ke a-ku a-i
Me Kona kai 'opua
Ke kai ma'o-ki'o-ki
Ke kai ma-li-no a o Kona
Ke kai ma-li-no a o Kona

LITERAL ENGLISH TRANSLATION
Famous are the calm waters of Kona
With the fluffy clouds on the horizon
From the slopes of the great
Mount Hualalai
To the peaceful seas of Kona.
We admire the strength of the young kane
As they glide the canoe
On the surface of the calm sea
With the distinguished clouds on the
horizon in Kona.
There's no other ocean area
can compare
With Kona and its fluffy clouds
Where the two changing currents meets.
In the calm seas of Kona.
In the calm seas of Kona.

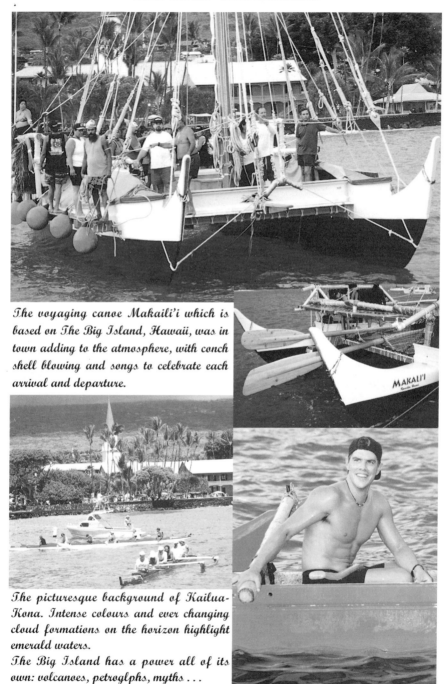

The voyaging canoe Makaili'i which is based on The Big Island, Hawaii, was in town adding to the atmosphere, with conch shell blowing and songs to celebrate each arrival and departure.

The picturesque background of Kailua-Kona. Intense colours and ever changing cloud formations on the horizon highlight emerald waters.
The Big Island has a power all of its own: volcanoes, petroglphs, myths ...

162

Some of the many radiant faces that bless this event and help to make it what it is. The spirit of aloha and ohana pervade. Bring your address book!

Below, Lanikai men Koa division, eventual winners overall ahead of Outrigger Canoe Club. They hit out in front early and stayed there taking an inside course and avoiding the strong currents.

Honaunau Bay – The Place of Refuge – the women's crews race down the coast from Kailua to finish here then exchange canoes with the waiting men. What a sight this is. Jammed with canoes, paddlers, colour and atmosphere, all set off by the irridescence of the water, tall coconut trees and the heat of tropical air.

Club Kai E Hitu. Take a short drive out of town towards the airport and you can find one of the best examples of a Koa canoe in the Hawaiian Islands.

A club with a proud, strong Tahitian connection and a belief in the traditional values of the sport of Va'a.

Tahitians jammed here for five hours after the race, with their eukele's, drums and songs of the islands.

Rush hour after the men's race at the King Kam' Hotel. The level of co-operation by club members and the way in which canoes are carried, rigged and de-rigged highlights one of the most important aspects of this sport – teamwork and support.

Hawaiian kids play like dolphins around the canoes, in a setting that could be Tahiti or Samoa. There is a magic to this place – Pu'uhonua O Honaunau – this place of refuge, a sanctuary for the ancient Hawaiians, a place for a second chance at life itself. A place where defeated warriors and kapu breakers could find refuge and escape death.

Blue waters, paddlers, Hawaiian, American, Canadian, Tahitian, Micronesian, canoes, paddles, iako, ama, leis, hugs, kisses, handshakes, shakas, hats, sunglasses, smiles, tatoos, bare feet, sand between your toes ...

Below: Teams from Micronesia – the island of Guam, a traditional stronghold of outrigger canoes and now becoming ever more involved in the sport.

The pier at Kailua-Kona. Lots of lovely ladies waiting for the men! Canoes cross the line for well over an hour to shouts and blasts from hooters. Flags fly and banners display club names. Leis are draped on finishing crews and the atmosphere builds for the evening's festivities.

This is not a rough water race, but rather a chance for all to participate in something quite special. Not so much a challenge of mind and body, but more a chance to celebrate outrigger canoe racing, its people and its very existence.

Race director Mike Atwood. This guy deserves a medal for all the work he puts in and still finds time to paddle in this, the largest long distance outrigger canoe race on the planet. This year, one hundred and twenty-seven men's crews on the start line which, as a matter of fact, had to be over two miles long! Crews so far away as to be barely visible. They tell me there was once a recall of the start – it took fifteen minutes just to stop people paddling.

Kailua's battle with Outrigger Hawaii was of epic proportions for most of the way. Outrigger led only to be overtaken as Honaunau Bay came into view. Outrigger put in the big efforts and Kisi Haine managed to steer them onto a few small runners to make up ground. Then it became a dog fight which resulted in Kailua on the rocks – not the drink, the team, or at least, their canoe. Both came to a halt then resumed the race with Outrigger outpowering Kailua in the final stretch, setting a new race record in a Koa canoe.

Wahine Wa'a Kaulau race finishes at Keahou, five and a half miles from Kailua. More colour, more atmosphere. I am reliably told this race is good for clearing hangovers.

Below, Kane Wa'a Kaulau. racing back to Kailua. Nice timing boys!

*Above Kailua women.
Right Outrigger OCC.
Black rock, blue sky,
and emerald waters.
Blow holes boom in
loud unison as waves
rush in from places
unknown.*

*Presentation songs and dance. An
Hawaiian plate lunch all washed down
with Gatorade & Rum cocktails. Bliss!*

Catalina-California

The thirty-first staging of the Catalina to Newport Beach Marathon took me somewhat by surprise, not by virtue of its epic proportion, but rather by the lack of it. This is not to say that the event is not a good one. It is. But there was a certain low key element which I had not expected.

The event was sponsored by Bacardi Rum and is hosted annually by the Offshore Canoe Club of Newport Beach, California. It is sanctioned by the Kalifornia Outrigger Association (KOA) of southern California and marks the end of the outrigger season.

Santa Catalina Island is located some twenty-nine miles off the coast of California, southwest of Newport Beach and separated from the mainland by the San Pedro Channel. The island was first associated with American Indians, followed by the Spanish and more recently made famous by the Wrigley empire (of chewing gum fame) when that family purchased the island to establish an offshore casino.

Today Catalina Island is a weekend getaway for stressed-out inhabitants of LA and others looking for a change of pace and perhaps a breath of fresh ocean air. Zane Grey, the author/adventurer made his home here where he popularised game fishing. Avalon, the main town, is reminiscent of an old time fishing village with quaint shops full of souvenirs and also a large number of eating and drinking spots.

The race course across the San Pedro Channel is traditionally thought of as a flat water race. Race divisions include Wahine and Kane in Malia, HCRA and IPCF canoe classes and a Masters over thirty-five, as well as for the Kane a Senior Master Men over forty-five division, with prizes awarded from first through to fourth.

The Wahine (women's) race is about twenty-seven miles, beginning at the Orange County Harbour Department and ending at Casino Point on Catalina. The Kane (men) race back the following day, thirty-one miles starting at Lover's Cove and finishing at Newport Dunes.

In past years, the men have raced to Catalina on Saturday with the women racing back to Newport Beach on Sunday. However due to a history of great thirst and over-abundance of hormonal energy causing the town of Avalon to buckle under intensive pressure of heavy-duty partying the race order was altered – women racing there and men racing back. Unfortunately, this has made a serious dent in what was a highlight of the event in the past.

I had travelled to the island prepared to follow the Kane back. Saturday was spent in eager anticipation of the arrival of the Wahine who had departed Newport Beach at 7.30am. You would have been hard pressed to know there was an event on, save for a few banners and outrigger tee-shirted individuals brandishing paddles. It

wasn't until around lunchtime and the arrival of the first women's crews that the atmosphere started to build.

The ocean was calm and glassy with a clear sky. The first crew to appear on the lazy horizon was California's Offshore followed by Outrigger Hawaii, followed by a large gap. The crossing had been predictably smooth and the finish seemed something of an anti-climax with a distinct lack of any fanfare.

As a gradual procession of canoes crossed the line accompanied by support boats, the scene congested with the atmosphere in the harbour and along the rock wall at Casino Point beginning to reach some sort of peak.

From out on the water I could see around to Descanso Beach which appeared to be going off so I decided to make haste to the shore there. Now being an English resident of Oz, and having spent long hours on beaches all around the planet, the use of the word "beach" in this instance struck me as a bit of an exaggeration.

I was further staggered when some

Team Offshore Canoe Club just hangin' around after the race.

Camping out at Descanso Beach seems the best way to get into the swing of things – after all, sleeping beside your canoe is the traditional thing to do!

lunatic asked me for $1.50 for the privilege of stepping on to its surface, elevating my perceptions to even more ludicrous proportions. I convinced him that I had travelled many miles on official business to photograph this world famous shore and he conceded to let my feet touch the ground – he was crazier than he looked.

It was all worth it, however, as I had finally stumbled into the epicentre of the event. This was obviously base camp for canoes and a camp ground for many paddlers. I made a mental note to camp out next time as this is without doubt a necessary part of really getting into the swing of things.

Canoes were paddled from the finish around to Descanso Beach and the difficult and painful task of carrying them over pebbles whilst avoiding slippery kelp under foot made an entertaining scene.

Then the Wahine were ready to party, relax and unwind, but by the cruel twist of altered race format the Kane for once

Malia division winners – Dana Point OCC California

Outrigger Canoe Club Hawaii arriving at Avalon in second spot behind Offshore.

ignored the plaintiff cries of women wanting badly to be entertained. The partying would have to wait.

Race day for the men and the ocean was calm and glassy with a one to two foot southwest swell. A clear sky, water temperature in the high sixties (about the same as the English Channel in summer I thought to myself) and air temperature in the mid-seventies completed the picture. Flat though the San Pedro Channel is, there are currents aplenty and this is where the race is won or lost. The steerer's decision as to course and the degree to which homework has been done are crucial.

Given past performances, local California team Dana Point were certainly considered favourites to win, with the likes of Outrigger Canoe Club of Hawaii and Hawaii Canoe & Kayak Team being strong contenders. California club Imua had recruited Olympic paddler Greg Barton and Offshore had their usual share of stars.

After a false start the race was underway and immediately many crews headed off in an easterly direction. The bulk of the pack stayed on a rum line for Newport. HCKT bolted in their usual fashion followed by Outrigger, Lanakila and Offshore, with Dana taking a different

course, leaving the other gun crews toughing it out amongst themselves.

Dana's slightly higher northerly course put them at the edge of the pack. Their tactic paid off immediately with an enormous lead within only forty minutes of the race. To the amazement of the other crews, this appeared to be at one stage as

The entrance to Newport Harbour and does it get exciting in here – obstacles aplenty keep steerers on task to the very end with many expensive distractions for rubber necks. Outrigger Canoe Club Hawaii.

much as a mile and a half.

Outrigger, who had headed a little east of the rum line found themselves in about sixth with other crews such as Imua. From there it was all uphill with Dana out in front. By the time the harbour entrance was reached, Outrigger had pulled into second spot and reduced Dana's lead to a half mile, followed closely by Lanakila and HCKT. Dana's move had paid off and their race was won within the first half hour.

The final leg up through the Newport Harbour waterway was as could be expected – hectic with week-enders doing their thing. The channel is a safe place to be when compared with the madness here!

The finish was much like the women's, somewhat anti-climactic. After their big effort, weary paddlers finished up at a small inlet where a few spectators greeted them – no leis or welcoming party, no music or announcements. Canoes were unrigged and trailered before prize giving in a nearby park. The laid-back California approach to outrigger canoe racing.

Lanakila finished third – another strong California crew.

Olapa Uila
"FLASH OF LIGHTNING"

Glass Off! Imua in the blue and paddling a Pacific Islander Canoe.

KOA/Catalina History

The Kalifornia Outrigger Canoe Association dates back to 1959 with the first race being held on September 20th, a distance race from Avalon on Catalina Island to Newport Dunes on the California coast.

In 1958, Albert Edward "Toots" Minvielle (founder of the now famous Moloka'i Hoe) had a chance meeting with Tommy Zahn from Santa Monica who had just paddled the Kaiwi Channel on a surfboard. Toots consulted Tommy about the possibility of introducing competitive outrigger canoe racing to California and Tommy responded by arranging a meeting in early 1959 with Tra David, the owner of Newport Dunes, Sam Miller, Commodore of Balboa Bay club and Al Oberg, Harbour Master of Newport Beach. As a result of that meeting, California's outrigger canoe racing began.

Duke Kahanamoku served as the Grand Marshall of the first California outrigger event and so the Catalina to Newport Dunes race was founded – the original California Outrigger Classic. This first race involved two canoes shipped to California via the efforts of Toots Minvielle. Both were Koa canoes with the names Malia (newcomer) and Niube (shark). The Malia crew consisted of an Hawaiian all star crew arranged by Toots who went on to win the race in five hours, while the newly formed California team in Niube finished only eleven minutes behind.

Lorrin Harrison, steerer and original member of the Niube crew recalls "When I first heard about canoe racing here, I had a dugout canoe that I had built in 1950. We were surfing it down in Doheny. Noah Kalama came by, he knew my sister from Hawaii and I knew him from body surfing. He asked if I could get a team of guys together who would like to paddle and race against a Hawaiian team. Of course I agreed. So we started coming here to the Dunes, paddling til nine every night. There were about fifteen paddling. Others would build a fire and we'd stay and paddle when the wind was howling. We worked for two months until we were sick of paddling in the same place. I though we would never get out in

Spring 1996

Outrigger Equipment
call 541-855-9686
fax 541-855-9041
Gold Hill Oregon USA

Race Chronology

1959	First race. Two Koa canoes. Won by Hawaiian all star crew.
1960-70	Hawaii competes and wins all races. Eight California clubs listed.
1971-76	Imua (Newport) wins.
1973	Last Catalina before a lay-off.
1977	Tahiti wins Marina Del Ray-Newport Race (fifty-two miles)
1978	Blazing Paddles wins Moloka'i. (Billy Whitford steerer)
1979	Balboa Bay Outrigger Canoe Club formed and became instrumental in restoring the Catalina race. Balboa won the Marina Del Ray - Huntington Harbour race (thirty-four miles).
1980	First race for women to Catalina from the Queen Mary. Hawaii competed. First Imua men, Offshore women.
1981-83	Imua men, Offshore women.
1984	First international teams in Catalina race. Tahiti first overall, first Malia division. Offshore women. Start of IPCF class racing.
1985	Imua men, Offshore women.
1986	Tahiti men, Offshore women.
1987	Imua men, Offshore women. Canada competes for first time.
1988	Imua men, Offshore women.
1989-90	San Diego men, Offshore women.
1991	Outrigger Hawaii men, Offshore women.
1992	Lanikai (Hawaii) men, Offshore women.
1993	Outrigger Hawaii men, Offshore women.
1994	Dana Point men, Outrigger Hawaii women.
1995	Dana Point men, Offshore women.

Crew numbers have now reached as many as sixty-five including teams from Hawaii, Tahiti, Canada, Texas, Arkansas, Wisconsin, Northern California, New Zealand and England.

to the ocean. Finally, Noah let us out and it was rough outside too. That's the way it all started right here in these Newport Dunes."

Noah Kalama, sent to California by Toots Minvielle to coach the first outrigger team there and Tom Johnson an original member of the first team, were the first to see the need for California-based canoes. The borrowed canoes used for that inaugural Catalina race were to be shipped back to Hawaii after the race, so Noah and Tom, realising that the development of the sport in California depended on local canoe manufacture, made a mould of the Malia hull. And so canoe building in California was born.

Moloka'i 1995

Within outrigger canoeing's ancient origins and association with the cultures of Oceania, there is indeed magic in the many stories of myth and legend. Bliss can be gained in the sensation and exhilaration of being upon the ocean and in the feeling of aliveness and wellbeing as you learn to interact harmoniously with nature's elements. Victory in challenging the ocean and yourself and triumphing. Power, gained physically and mentally, in being your best. Celebration in overcoming challenge and in being a part of all that outrigger canoe paddling embraces – friendship, health and an affinity with the ocean environment. And religion, as outrigger canoeing has become a way of life for thousands of people, having the power to make a believer out of you; to see the world around you in a different light; allowing you to associate with those of like mind who understand the physical, mental and spiritual implications of participating in an ancient sport.

**A symbolic offering greets the Hale O Lono Dawn.
Another Moloka'i . . . another challenge of mind, body and spirit.**

Bankoh
Na Wahine O Ke Kai

Offshore Goes Off Again!

This year the top seven crews beat Offshore's 1990 record, but six of them still didn't beat Offshore . . .

For the seventeenth annual Bankoh Na Wahine O Ke Kai a record forty-nine teams lined up (two more than '94) indicative of the popularity and growth of women's participation in outrigger canoe racing.

No doubt about it, the Na Wahine O Ke Kai belongs to California's Offshore Canoe Club, with nine victories out of the last ten crossings and this the third straight win (Outrigger Canoe Club won in 1992). The big question now is, who is going to knock them off their perch? For the moment they're nailed there – super-glued in place it would seem.

Nevertheless it was a good year for many crews in as much the first seven finishers bettered Offshore's 1990 record of 5:44:13, with conditions being described by Offshore steerer, Mindy Clarke as *simply the best of paddling conditions – moderate waves and favourable wind and current.*

Offshore finished the crossing in 5:24:42 bettering their record by almost twenty minutes. The 1990 record was set using twelve paddlers, a ruling which was changed to ten in 1994.

Offshore's crew included Mindy Clarke, Sharon Attlesley, Gina Aubrey, Sheila Conover, Dru Van Hengel, Vicki Mills, Jo-Jo Toeppner, Cathy Ho Whitford and from Sweden, two kayakers Agenta Andersson and Anna Olsson who between them have eight Olympic kayak medals.

Despite Offshore's win, coach Billy Whitford appreciates that the level of competitiveness is growing with the passing of each season and that the odds are now running against Offshore maintaining their dominance. *Crews were on our stern much of the way, not once could I relax. I don't look for Offshore to dominate forever.*

Crews from Outrigger Hawaii, Kailua and Lanikila (California) made sure Offshore worked for their victory. The start was anything but clean, with several canoes becoming entangled including Outrigger which then had to work hard to make time up and also Kailua who were spun around a hundred and eighty degrees when struck in the tail by another canoe. As Kisi Haine of Outrigger said . . . *it didn't affect the finish so much, but it plays a role mentally. It was so stressful. Everybody was screaming.*

Offshore and Lanikila broke away early at the start, followed closely by Outrigger and Kailua, but by the first change-over near Laau Point, Offshore began to nudge ahead. Two hours into the race and Outrigger and Kailua both decided to make tactical moves rather than sticking with Offshore as they felt they couldn't catch them on hull speed alone. Outrigger headed on a northerly course, Offshore southerly and Kailua in between. By the time they were off Portlock on Oahu, Outrigger was lying about half a mile behind Offshore and Kailua farther back than this. Once at Portlock and heading down around Diamond Head, it was just a question of working the runners and Offshore's victory was complete.

Aerial perspective of form and function. Hale O Lono Harbour. The 1995 Bankoh Na Wahine O Ke Kai and Moloka'i Hoe attracted record numbers of entrants, proof positive of the growing attraction to outrigger canoe racing and the challenges that it offers. Forty-nine women's crews and ninety-two men's crews – over twelve hundred paddlers – made the crossing.

Kisi Haine, steerer for Outrigger Hawaii, said that *Offshore's women were too strong, too powerful. Our crew was good and our boat fast, but we were no match for Offshore's speed.*

Outrigger finished second in 5:31:09, Kailua third in 5:36, California's Lanikila fourth in 5:41:04 and Kai Opua from the Big Island fifth.

In the Koa division, Waikiki Surf won in 5:51:43, ninth overall, whilst Maui Masters (over 35) 5:53:51 and Koa Kai Senior Masters (over 45) 6:24:01 won their respective divisions.

Original Wahine Crew Crosses the Channel Once Again

On a nostalgic note, twenty six years after the first Kaiwi Channel crossing by women's crews, eighteen of the original women paddled together in the event again.

With eighteen members, the crew could not be considered for a placing in the Senior Masters division which allows only twelve paddlers. However this consideration was not their primary concern – it was to be a reunion of friends, a chance to tackle personal challenge and relive that first crossing.

The seventeenth annual crossing was dedicated to the original thirty-six women who paddled in a total of two crews (Healani and

179

Onipaa) back in 1975. In that year they proved their point in an otherwise male dominated sport, that women could take on and complete the crossing of one of the world's most unpredictable and dangerous open ocean channels.

Since that time women's participation in outrigger canoeing across the Pacific and beyond has flourished and their achievements back then certainly had a strong influence on the way that its popularity has spread.

In 1995 many of this crew were over fifty years of age, and comprised of members of both the original teams including Evelyn Arakaki, Bozo Bell, Shay Bintliff, Georgia Campbell, Queenie Goo, Alohalani Jamais, Mali Meyer, Bernie Nii, Ellen Pabliano, Robin Reed, Ui Bell, Sammie Teixeira, Anona Napolean, Lilinoe Farias, Jan Davies and Florence Apa (who at sixty-five was the oldest member).

Hana Hou (to do again) as they called themselves, finished in 6:37:58.

Lanikai Restores Hawaiian Pride!

Not since 1990 has the prestigious Bankoh Moloka'i Hoe been won by an Hawaiian club. Jim Foti's thoughts on this year's win were: *We brought the trophy back to Hawaii where it belongs. We also returned pride to our Lanikai community.*

Lanikai Men's crew was awesome all throughout the '95 season but many thought that the Moloka'i event would perhaps see some of the nuts and bolts fall off and leave the path open for other rough water downhill specialists like Outrigger Canoe Club and Tahiti. But not so, their

Lanikai Smokin' Home . . .

Shipping canoes to the island of Moloka'i and transporting them by truck to Hale O Lano Harbour. Getting paddlers to the island. Having the canoes rigged, weighed, measured, numbered and registered. Then the logistics of race day itself. Each and every one of the officials and organisers deserve recognition for their efforts every time they make it happen. It is getting harder for them not easier, with each passing year. To all of them from all of us, Mahalo Nui Loa!

performance was nothing short of brilliant, revelling in the rough water conditions and on the day many would say they were unbeatable by any crew from anywhere!

At the end of the day local paddlers were glad to see that it had been won by a Hawaiian crew, irrespective of which crew it was. But Lanikai also did it in style in a time of 4:53:03, bettering the 1993 record set by the Tahitian Faa'a crew of 4:55:27 by 2:24. This was to be Lanikai's first Moloka'i victory since 1974 and did they have fun doing it. . .*We caught some fabulous surfing rides, where our entire crew screamed and shouted for more* said John Foti, *Conditions in the channel were perfect with currents, twenty-five knot winds and swells of six to ten feet pushing us along – and we didn't make any mistakes this year. In previous years, we made a lot of mistakes that always seemed to cost us.* Steerer, and John's brother, Jim Foti said *We've been trying to get this for the past seven, eight years and we've stuck together all those years. We easily could have gone and paddled for other crews, but we wanted to win it together.*

The atmosphere on the eve of the race was made all the more tense with strong trade winds blowing, rain squalls and a forecast of twelve to eighteen foot swells in the channel.

If you have never paddled across the Kaiwi Channel – let alone seen what it can be like – you need to be aware that this blue stretch of water is totally unpredictable, with strong currents and the potential for immense ocean and wind energy. There's only one way to go when you have committed yourself to a canoe ride home to

Kai Opua OCC. Moloka'i in the background.

the tourist laden shores of Waikiki. The weather can't be put on hold. What it serves up you've gotta swallow. Don't think you're gonna get lucky and have them cancel the race! The point here is, commitment to this race has to be one hundred percent and demands that you *be prepared.*

A sleepless night was had by all, with the trades trying to uproot palm trees and driving rain beating against bedroom windows. By the time we climbed onto buses for the bumpy trip to Hale O Lono, it wasn't much better.

The race got off to a reasonable start, with a record ninety-two crews of which eighty-eight were to finish. But if the start

was clean the real trouble was about to begin. The first crew change is not allowed before thirty minutes which puts the top crews at the tip of the island off Laau Point.

Tension builds at this point as support boats loaded with relief paddlers and coaches are itching to plant the throttle and go looking for their canoe to give support and make the first change. Support boats hugged close to the lead boat – and the tension mounted with all boat drivers looking for the go ahead.

Finally (and I make no judgment as to what seemed to happen from my vantage point on the lead boat) a few boats crept farther and farther ahead until apparently a

signal was given to go. After the event it was deemed that at that time there had still been ten seconds to go and that the necessary signal had not been given. Who knows? And in the end for the sake of ten seconds in the scheme of things, who cares!

Unfortunately the race committee did care and decided to penalize the ten teams that allegedly took off. About an hour after the finish a ten minute penalty was imposed on the ten leading crews. In fairness, this was not going to work, as no accurate account of who the "breakaways" were seemed to be at hand because support boats do not carry identification – maybe they should – and no one had been keeping a record. With respected paddlers such as Walter Guild denying that his team (Outrigger) was one of the boats involved in the hands of one Hawaii's best boat drivers Greg Moss, it was going to be a tough call to pull off.

Half an hour later the penalties were

lifted although meetings were held over subsequent days to try to resolve the issue. *It didn't change the outcome of the race at all. I don't think it should change the outcome of history either* said Jim Foti. And Lanikai paddler, Kalani Irvine's comment – *Did anyone gain an advantage by doing that? I don't think so. I don't think any of those teams were out there doing it intentionally and I don't think it affected the rest of the race.*

For all of the crossing Lanikai dominated, taking a marginally northerly course, with Fa'aa south of them and Outrigger to the north of them. Fa'aa remained the only contender with Lanikai

Below: Tahiti's support vessel and relief crew at the start before the controversy and at right, Greg Moss who throughout the year helped me to get some great shots with his fine boat handling skills.

Koa Division Winners. Outrigger

Mooloolaba Masters . . . again. Another division in which the Hawaiians are keen to regain domination.

Tahiti runners up. If French Polynesia had a salt mine, that's where these guys would end up! Indicative of the level of national pride associated with their success or failure.

for most of the way, whilst Outrigger made its move towards the end of the race with Todd Bradley taking an inside course following the Oahu shoreline early on and this way gaining a lot of ground on Fa'aa who were still making their way across on the southerly course.

The Tahitian crew, once again steered by Tom Connor, finished second in a time of 5:01:39. Tom's comment: *You can talk about the conditions and the canoes and all that, but the bottom line is that the best team wins the race. The best team won on this day, we didn't paddle well enough to win.*

Outrigger Canoe Club Hawaii placed third in 5:03:00, fourth was Waikiki Surf

Club 5:09:08 and fifth Outrigger Australia 5:10:56.

Australian Master Mens (over 35) crew paddled with four Hawaiians steered by Kenny Powell from Kailua-Kona and won their division for the second consecutive year. They finished in tenth place overall in 5:20:09, followed by Outrigger Canoe Club Hawaii 5:27:01 and Maui club Malama Ula 5:38:40.

The Koa division was won by Outrigger Canoe Club Hawaii in 5:36:23, followed by California's Lanikila 5:52:05 and Lanikai 6:14:57.

A Nike sponsored team from Hungary entered the event comprising of Olympic kayak paddlers and finished twenty-eighth

Just for the hell of it and a tribute to fine lines and curvatures . . .

overall. Their manager works for Nike in Hungary and is a past resident of Hawaii. They have purchased a canoe which is to be left in Hawaii and plan to return each year.

Lanikai's crew consisted of the two Foti brothers Jim and John, Rich Lambert, Bob Nottage, Rocky Owens, Bo Eastabrook, Kalani Irvine, Mike Smith and Mike Pedersen many of whom have paddled for the club since they were ten year olds.

The Tahitian road crew never ends a race without a jam session

In the beginning there was
no land, no light, only darkness
and the vast ocean where earth-maker
and great grandfather were
afloat in their canoe.

creation myth

Full Color Poster 24x28 inches.
In the trough during the 62 mile Moorea Race,
French Polynesia.

Photographer: Daphne Hougard.

"Changing Boats"

A PHOTOGRAPHIC COLLECTION

Works by photographer Daphne
Hougard document her twelve year
study of outrigger canoes. • Daphne's
passion has led her through the South
Pacific, Hawaii, California and Canada,
where she has covered four world
championships. Her most recent work
has been the documentation of the
outrigger canoe's role in traditional village life in the Tokelau Islands. • "I race
as a crew member in these boats myself, and I want to illustrate the cultural
heritage of this ancient vessel through its place in sport today." There may be
no other sport to match the antiquity of outrigger canoeing, and it is a sport
that is capturing the imagination of an ever growing, enthusiastic following.

Full color photographic prints available from size 8"x10" to 30"x40"

"Amazon Paddler"

"Uhane Canoe"

"Blessing the Canoes"

"Transfer"

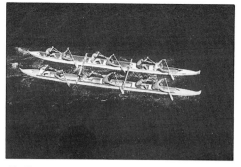

"6x6"

Full color
photographic
prints available
from size
8"x10" to
30"x40"

"Outrigger Under Sail"

"Silkscreen"

"Splash Down"

 # Outrigger Order Form

Print & Poster Prices

8"x10"	$25.00
11"x14"	35.00
16"x20"	50.00
30"x40"	130.00
Posters	20.00

(Outrigger Canoe Racing Poster 24"x28")

ALL 8X10 - 30X40 SIZES ARE COLOR PHOTOGRAPHIC PRINTS

QTY.	SIZE	TITLE OF PRINT	PRICE

Include an additional $5.00 for a complete full color catalog.	Shipping	$5.50 USD
	Total Due	

Please allow up to 20 days for delivery of order.

Name _____

Address _____

_____

Phone_____

Send Check or Money Order to:
(U.S. Dollars or equivalent.)

Daphne Hougard
20A Sunnyside Ave, Suite 151
Mill Valley, California 94941 USA
Telephone (415) 381-0733

The Kanu Shop

The Kanu Shop

Embroidered Ka'nu Culture Hats & Shirts

Air Freighted Worldwide. Prices shown in Australian dollars. Please pay equivalent.

Ka'nu Culture Hat	navy blue ❑ royal blue ❑	$15
Ka'nu Culture T-shirt	navy blue ❑ royal blue ❑ L ❑ XL ❑	$20
Ka'nu Culture Polo Shirt	navy blue ❑ royal blue ❑ L ❑ XL ❑	$28
Ka'nu Culture Patch	navy blue	$8

* Gold & Turquoise embroidery on all items. Hats add $3 p&p in Australia – $5 OverSeas. Shirts add $5, O/S $8. Patch $1.50, O/S $3.

Enclosed please find my cheque, money order, bank draft for $

Please charge my: Visa Card ◯   Mastercard ◯   Bankcard ◯

signature   expiry date

name   phone

address

BATINI BOOKS PO BOX 506 MAROOCHYDORE AUSTRALIA Q 4558

Kanu Culture Volume I Air Freighted Worldwide.

Please send me a copy of Ka'nu Culture Vol I $15 (Aust) or equivalent. ❑
Add $3 p&p in Australia. $8 overseas.

Enclosed please find my cheque, money order, bank draft for $

Please charge my: Visa Card ◯   Mastercard ◯   Bankcard ◯

signature   expiry date

name   phone

address

BATINI BOOKS PO BOX 506 MAROOCHYDORE AUSTRALIA Q 4558

Hawaiian Canoe Book

Australia, Fiji, New Zealand, some neighbouring islands $55 (Aust) or equivalent. $6 p&p in Australia. $12 overseas.

Enclosed please find my cheque, money order, bank draft for $

Please charge my: Visa Card ◯   Mastercard ◯   Bankcard ◯

signature   expiry date

name   phone

address

BATINI BOOKS PO BOX 506 MAROOCHYDORE AUSTRALIA Q 4558

Planet Outrigger

American Samoa

Every effort has been made to ensure these contact addresses are correct as at January '96. Updated addresses mailed, emailed, or faxed to us during the year would be very much appreciated. Apologies for any errors or omissions. Ed.

AMERICAN SAMOA CANOE RACING ASSOCIATION

BOX 1757 PAGO PAGO AMERICAN SAMOA

Australia

AUSTRALIAN OUTRIGGER CANOE RACING ASSOCIATION

BOX 506, MAROOCHYDORE Q 4558 PH/FAX (074) 79 1327

NEW SOUTH WALES ZONE

BOX 941 BROOKVALE BUSINESS CENTRE NSW 2100

Bilgola OCC PO Box 43, Avalon Beach NSW 2107

Cape Byron OCC 2 Byron St, Bangalow NSW 2479

Coogee OCC 2 Denning St, Coogee NSW 2034

Manly-Warringah Kayak Club PO Box 58, Newport NSW 2106

Nine Mile OCC 27A Violet Town Rd,Tingira Hts, Newcastle NSW 2290

Pacific OCC 33 Alfred St, Mascot NSW 2020

Pittwater OCC

Port Hacking OCC PO Box 101, Caringbah NSW 2229

St George OCC PO Box 94, Oatley NSW 2223

Sydney OCC 771 Military Rd, Mosman NSW 2088

QUEENSLAND, NORTHERN ZONE

4 CHARLES STREET CRANBROOK Q 4814

Bowen OCC PO Box 413, Bowen Q4805

Cairns Beaches OCC PO Box 31, Palm Cove Q4879

Capricorn Coast OCC PO Box 1068, Yeppoon Q 4703

Magnetic Island Boat Club Coral Sea PO Box 76, Nelly Bay Q4819

Hamilton Island OCC PO Box 49, Hamilton Island Q4803

Hayman Island OCC via Airlie Beach Q4802

Hay Point OCC PO Box 124, Sarina Q4747

Mackay OCC PO Box 696, Mackay Q4740

Magnetic Island OCC PO Box 937, Hyde Park Q4812

Malihini OCC 36 Coral Esp, Cannonvale Q4802

Outrigger Whitsunday PO Box 158, Cannonvale Q4802

Port Douglas OCC PO Box 42, Port Douglas Q4871

Raging Thunder OCC PO Box 299, Mission Beach Q4854

Reef City OCC PO Box 1956, Gladstone Q4680

Rockhampton OCC PO Box 5661, Rockhampton MC Q4702

Slade Point OCC PO Box 3189, Mackay Q4740

Sunset Bay OCC PO Box 8337, Mt Pleasant Q4740

Townsville OCC PO Box 1946, Townsville Q4810

QUEENSLAND, SOUTHERN ZONE

30 CORONET CRES BURLEIGH WATERS Q 4220

Brisbane OCC Inc PO Box 553, Bulimba, Brisbane Q4171

Canoe Point Outriggers Inc 5 Currawong Crt, Boyne Island Q4680

East Coast OCC PO Box 415, Virginia Q4014

Fraser Coast OCC PO Box 1089, Pialba Q4655

Mooloolaba OCC PO Box 763, Mooloolaba Q4557

Noosa OCC Inc PO Box 137, Noosaville Q4566

Northcliffe OCC 30 Coronet Cres, Burleigh Waters Q4220

Oceania OCC Inc PO Box 533, Buddina Q4575

Outrigger Canoe Club of Australia Inc 6/99 Seagull Ave, Mermaid Beach Q4218

Panamuna OCC Inc PO Box 925, Mooloolaba Q4557

Surfers Paradise OCC PO Box 6305, Gold Coast MC, Bundall Q4217

Taimanu OCC Inc PO Box 6728, Gold Coast MC Q4217

Tweed Heads Rowing & Aquatic Club 72 Warringa Dr, Bilambil Hts NSW 3486

WESTERN AUSTRALIA

11 MAYNARD PDE, GELORUP WA 6230

California

KALIFORNIA OUTRIGGER ASSOCIATION

PO BOX 66-626, LOS ANGELES CA 90066 PH (310) 338 1290

Blackie's

Dana 22542 Paseo La Vista, Laguna Nigel CA 92677

Hanohano 2061 Wilbur Ave, San Diego CA 92109

Hokuloa PO Box 23265, Ventura CA 93302

Imua 73 La Perla, Foothill Ranch CA 92610

Kahakai 2508 E. Willow #210, Signal Hill CA 90806

Kai Elua 3607 Ocean Front Walk #1A, San Diego CA 92109

Ka Nai A 1505 San Leandro Lane, Santa Barbara CA 93108

Kumulani 4748 50th St, San Diego CA 92115

Lanakila 839 1/2 Lucia Ave, Redondo Beach CA 90277

Marina 12627 Gilmore St, Los Angeles CA 90066

Nahoa 2209 W. 180th St, Torrance CA 90504

Newport 20232 Orchid St, Costa Mesa CA 92627

Offshore 221 23rd St, Costa Mesa CA 92627

Santa Barbara 1311 De la Guerra St, Santa Barbara CA 93101

San Diego 3222 Eichenlaub St, San Diego CA 92117

NORTHERN CALIFORNIA OUTRIGGER CANOE ASSOCIATION

643 CORNELL AVE, SALINAS CA 93901 FAX (408) 899 1368

Akau Hana c/- 1745 47th Ave #1, Capitola CA 95010

Benicia Canoe Club 1120 El Dorado St, Valejo CA 94590

Hui O'Hawaii of Sacramento 1804 Edgemont Way, Roseville CA 95678

Hui Wa'a O'San Jose 47 N Temple Dr #4, Milpitas CA 95035

Kahekili O' Ke Kai PO Box 25364, San Mateo CA 94402

Kai Ku'Ono 1612 S Sacremento St, Lodi CA 95240

Kaimanu 1217 139th Ave, San Leandro CA 94578

Kamali'i O' Ke Kai 325 Union Ave #160B Campbell CA 95008

Ke Anuenue 3688 Norfolk, Fremont CA 94538

Ke Kai O'Uhane 500 Glenwood Circle #424, Monterey CA 93940

Kilo Hana 43088 Evergaldes Pk Dr, Fremont CA 94538

Koa Kai 1622 Boston St, Salinas CA 93905

Lokahi 1304 McDowell Blvd, Petaluma CA 94954

Na Mea Wa'a O'Kapalakiko 768 Bounty Dr #6805, Foster City CA 94404

Naleo O'Ke Kai 2413 Joseph Court East, Santa Rosa CA 95407

O'Kalani 2704 Central Ave, Alameda CA 94501

Pu Pu O'Hawaii 1031 Clyde Ave #901, Santa Clara CA 95050

Canada

CANADIAN OUTRIGGER REGIONAL ASSOCIATION

False Creek (604) 730 7890

Jericho (604) 984 6861

Lotus (604) 873 2115

Whistler (604) 938 3350

Cook Islands (Raratonga)

COOK ISLANDS CANOE ASSOCIATION

PO BOX 108 RAROTONGA COOK ISLANDS

The Fiji Islands

FIJI OUTRIGGER CANOE RACING ASSOCIATION

PO BOX 3084, LAMI, FIJI PH (679) 314 386 FAX 300 217

Denarau Canoe Club PO Box 441, Na

Hot Qitawa Canoe Club PO Box 5650, Lautok

Nausori Canoe Club PO Box 72, Na

Lami Kai Wai Canoe Club PO Box 3084, Lam

Fiji Navy Canoe Club PO Box 12387, Walu Bay, Suv

Takia Canoe Club PO Box 342, Suv

Guam & the Marianas Island

GUAM KAYAK & OUTRIGGER CANOE FEDERATION (PROA)

NOLAN HENDRICKS (671) 734 0490 FAX 734 6824

Manhala Outrigger Club c/- Primo Surf, Agana Shopping Center, Agana, Guar

MARIANAS PADDLESPORTS RACING ASSOCIATION (MPRA)

PO BOX ET, AGANA GUAM PH (671) 649 6772 FAX 649 5209

Paluman Tasi PO Box 12667 Tamuning Guam 9693

The Islands of Hawai

HAWAIIAN CANOE RACING ASSOCIATION

123 KAMEHAMEHA, HONOLULU HI 95999 PH (903) 123 4566 FAX 123 3344

GARDEN ISLAND CANOE RACING ASSOCIATION (KAUAI)

PO BOX 43 LIHUE HAWAII HI 96766

Hanalei Canoe Club PO Box 690 Kilauea HI 9675

Hui O Mana Ka Pu'uwai 3470 Lawailoa Lane, Koloa HI 9675

Kailoa Canoe Club PO Box 3616 Lihue, HI 9676

Kawaikini Canoe Club 323 Kamokila Rd, Kapaa HI 9675

Kilohana Canoe Club PO Box 1254 Koloa HI 9675

Koloa Canoe Club PO Box 1254 Koloa HI 9675

MOLOKA'I CANOE RACING ASSOCIATION

PO BOX 767, KAUNAKAKAI HI 96748

Ho'Opili Canoe Club PO Box 838 Kaunakakai HI 9674

Mana'E Canoe Club (inactive) PO Box 660 Kaunakakai HI 9674

Molokai Canoe Club PO Box438 Kaunakakai HI 9674

MAUI COUNTY HAWAIIAN CANOE ASSOCIATION

PO BOX 1224, KIHEI HI 96753

Hana Canoe Club 5011 Uakea Rd Hana HI 9671

Hawaiian Canoe Club PO Box 5098 Kahului HI 9673

Hui Na Pookela Canoe Club 260A Halenani Dr Wailuku HI 9679

Kahana Canoe Club PO Box 11604 Lahaina HI 96761

Kihei Canoe Club PO Box 741 Kihei HI 96761

Lae Ula O Kai 393 Front St Lahaina HI 96761

Lahaina Canoe Club 2435 Kaauapali Pkwy J Lahaina HI 96761

Na Kai 'Ewalu Canoe Club 795 Analio St Wailuku HI 96793

Napili Canoe Club 1506 Malo St Lahaina HI 96761

KU O HAWAII CANOE RACING ASSOCIATION

BOX 995, KAILUA-KONA HI 96745

Hilo Bay Canoe Club PO Box 210 Papaikou HI 96781

Kai-E-Hitu Canoe Club PO Box 1821 Kailua-Kona HI 96745

Kai Opua Canoe Club PO Box 3079 Kailua-Kona HI 96740

Kamehameha Canoe Club 486B Akolea St Hilo HI 96740

Kawaihae Canoe Club PO Box 856 Kamuela HI 96743

Keauhou O Kona Canoe Club PO Box 150 Kealakekua HI 96750

Keaukaha Canoe Club 35 Aheahe St Hilo HI 96720

Keoua Canoe Club PO Box 620 Honaunau HI 96726

Kona Athletic Club PO Box 63 Keahou HI 96739

Paiea Canoe Club 76-6270 Plumerian Rd Kailua- Kona HI 96740

Puna Canoe Club PO Box 594 Pahoa HI 96745

Queen Lilliuokalani Canoe Club PO Box 1532 Kailua-Kona HI 96745

Waikoloa Canoe Club PO Box 384287 Waikoloa HI 96738

Wailani Canoe Club 395 Todd Ave Hilo HI 96720

WAIIAN CANOE RACING ASSOCIATION

LUNAHELU ST, KAILUA, HI 96734

Anuenue Canoe Club 3334 Kauhana Pl, Honolulu HI 96816

Haleakala Canoe Club (inactive)

Healani Canoe Club 2457 a Kawohi Pl, Honolulu HI 96819

Honolulu Canoe Club 94-1097 Mele St Waipahu HI 96797

Hui Lanakila Canoe Club 3633 Sierra Dr Honolulu HI 96816

Hui Nalu Canoe Club 114 Lunalilo Home Rd Honolulu HI 96825

Kailua Canoe Club 1611 Uluamahi Pl Kailua HI 96734

Kai Oni Canoe Club 335 Auwinala Rd Kailua HI 96734

Ko'Olau Canoe Club 551 Iliaina St Kailua HI 96734

Lanikai Canoe Club 45 Kawailoa Rd #6, Kailua HI 96734

Leeward Kai Canoe Club 89-889 Nanakuli Av Waianae HI 96792

Makaha Canoe Club 87-266 Laulele St Waianae HI 96792

Outrigger Canoe Club 2909 Kalakaua Av Honolulu HI 96815

Surfsports 878 Kainui Dr Kailua HI 96734

Waikiki Surf Club 791 Sunset Av Honolulu HI 96816

Waianalo Canoe Club 407 N Kalaheo Av Kailua HI 96734

NA'OHANA O NA HUI WA'A INC (OAHU)

PO BOX 2279 HONOLULU HI 96804

Hawai'ian Outrigger Canoe Club PO Box 264 Kaneohe HI 96744

Hui O Ikaika 84-1065 Kaulawaha Rd Waianae Hi 96792

Kai Po'Ha Outrigger Canoe Club 99-510 Halawa Hts Rd Aiea HI 96701

Kalihi-Kai Canoe Club 2260 Kaululaau St Honolulu HI 96813

Kamehameha Canoe Club 1224 Alakapuna St #506 Honolulu HI 96744

Kaneohe Outrigger Canoe Club 45-412 Konale Pl Kaneohe HI 96744

Keala Canoe Club (inactive)

Koa Kai Canoe Club 1088 Bishop #2203 Honolulu HI 96813

Lokahi Canoe Club 1451 S King St #300 Honolulu HI 968414

Manu O Ke Kai 278-b Karsten Dr Wahiawa HI 96786

Na Keiki O Ka Mo'i Club 85-128 a Maiuu Rd Waianaehi 96792

Waikiki Beach Boys 47-150 a Hui Alaiaha Kaneohe HI 96744

Waikiki Yacht Club 4053 Likini St Honolulu HI 96818

Windward Kai Canoe Club 1454 Onioni St Kailua HI 96734

New Caledonia

LIQUE CALEDONIENNE DE PIROGUE POLYNESIAN

BP 3246 NOUMEA, NOUMEA, NEWCALEDONIA

As Pacifique Club (ASPC) 19 rue Albert Blum, 2ème secteur, rivière salée, 98800 Noumea

As Kanaky Rame (As Kara) Lot 505, rue Martin du Gard, Koutio 98830 Dumbea

Manutea Hui Va'a Club (As Manutéa) 23 rue Caulry, Ducos, 98800 Noumea

As PTT Noumea Section Va'a (As PTT) BP 3246, 98846 Noumea Cedex

As Sato 16 rue Gambetta, 1ère Valée du Tir, 98800 Noumea

As Jeunes Des Isles Sous le Vent (JISLV) 427 lotissement FSH, rue Romain Rolland, Koutio, 98800 Dumbea

Meherio Hoe Club (Méhério HC) BP 11936, Magenta, 98802 Noumea Cedex

Pirogue Club de Dumbea (PC Dumbéa) 440 rue Romain Rolland, Koutio, 98830 Dumbea

New Zealand - Aotearoa

NGA KAIHOE O AOTEAROA

AUCKLAND REGION OUTRIGGER CANOE ASSOCIATION

PB 93109, WAITAKERE, CITY AUCKLAND FAX (09) 836 8060

Akarana Dragons Sports Club PO Box 101117 Nth Shore Auckland

Hauraki Sports Club Inc PO Box 18370, Glenn Innes Auckland

Hawaiki Nui Tua Rua PO Box 75, Otaki

Hineauta Waka Ama Inc 44 Dalton St, Gisborne

Kaitaia Dolphins 16 Vegar St, Kaitaia

Kororaraka Wellington St, Russell, Bay of Islands

Manukau Outrigger Canoe Club 23 Ambury Rd, Mangere, Auckland

Marei-kura Outrigger Canoe Club 67 Endcliffe Rd, Gisborne

Mitamitaga O Le Pasefica Vaa'alo PO Box 371, Whangarei

Mulivai Outrigger Canoe Club 30 Thomas Rd, Mangere, Auckland

Nga Hoe Horo Outrigger Club RD2 Broadwood, Hokianga

Nga Tai Whakarongo Outrigger CC PO Box 6, Whatawhata Hamilton

Nga Tini Hoe O Anuiwaru Ki Porirua Waka Ama 21 Doncaster Tce, Ascot Park, Porirua

Nga Waka O Te Awa A Te Atua PO Box 6, Whatawhata

Ngati Kahu Te Pura 245 State Highway 2, Tauranga West

Okahu Bay Outrigger Canoe Club 52 Ngaio St, Orakei Auckland

Owhiuwa Waka-Ama Club 1 Tainui St, Onerahi, Wharangei

Pakinga Outrigger Canoe Club c/-269 Meola Rd, Pt Chevalier Auckland

Pineula Manurewa Outrigger Canoe Club 12 Christmas Rd, Manurewa

Tairawhiti Outrigger Canoe Club 239 Ormond Rd, Gisborne

Tai Tokerau Polynesian Canoe Assoc PO Box 371, Wharangei

Tamaki Outrigger Canoe Club 3 William Ave, One Tree Hill Auckland

Taniwha Outrigger & Dragon Boat CC 29 Hitchcock Cres, Paremoremo Albany

Tarawera Outrigger Canoe Club 8 Valley Rd, Kawerau

Tauranga Moana Outrigger Canoe Club 31 Carmichaels Rd, Tauranga

Te Awa Haku Outrigger Club PO Box 24269, Ch Ch

Te Waiariki Purea Waka Ama PO Box 95, Rotorua

Te Waka Hoe O Pokohinu Private Bag, Omaio

Te Whanau O Nga Waka 21 Regina St, Gray Lynn Auckland

Tsunami Dragon Sports Club 24 Cabello Place, Glenfield

Tu'Fu'Atasi 7A Stoke St, Newton, Wellington

Tu Nui A Te Ika 16 Nevey Rd, Mirimar, Wellingto

Tuatini Ki Uawa Outrigger CC Kowhai Tops Rd1 Tolaga Bay, East Coas

Wainui Outrigger Canoe Club PO Box 2108, Gisborn

Waitakere Longboat & Canoe Club Private Bag 93109, Henderso

Whangape Outrigger Club RD1, Herekino, Whangap

NEW ZEALAND OUTRIGGERS FEDERATION INC

8 CRAWFORD AVE MANGERE BRIDGE, AUCKLAND PH-/FAX (09) 622 1662

Oregon

OREGON RACING CANOE ASSOCIATION

15775 NE EILERS RD AURORA OR 97002 (503) 678 1440

Central Oregon Outrigger Canoe Club PO Box 5626, Bend OR 9770

Columbia River Outrigger Canoe Club PO Box 10903, Portland OR 9721

Mountain Home C C 21001 SW Mountain Home, Sherwood, OR 9714

Seattle Outrigger Canoe Club 14350 "A" 19th NE, Seattle, Washington 9812

Stevenson Canoe & Kayak Club PO Box 102, Stevenson Washington 98648

Rapa Nui - Easter Islands

MATA HOE VAKA KAHU KAHU O HERA RAPA NUI

(THE RAPA NUI OUTRIGGER CLUB)

c/ 3300 SWEETWATER MESA, MALIBU CA 90265 FAX (310) 456 8604

Stahlo Nation

STAHLO CANOE CLUB

Tahiti

FEDERATION TAHITIENNE DE VA'A

PAPAETTE, TAHITI

United Kingdom

ROYAL CANOE CLUB

3A SHAWFIELD ST CHELSEA LONDON SW3 4BA

Wallis-Futuna

Western Samoa

WESTERN SAMOA OUTRIGGER ASSOCATION

PO BOX 1666 APIA WESTERN SAMOA FAX (685) 23 636